MULTIMEDIA on *YOUR PC*

Francis Botto

SIGMA PRESS – Wilmslow, United Kingdom

CW01638697

093816 b

93816 bc
~~136920~~
NORTH EAST WORCESTERSHIRE
COLLEGE LIBRARY
005.75 BOT

Copyright ©, F. Botto, 1994

All Rights Reserved. No part of this publication may be reproduced, stored in a retrieval system, or transmitted in any form or by any means, electronic, mechanical, photocopying, recording or otherwise, without prior written permission.

First published in 1994 by

Sigma Press, 1 South Oak Lane, Wilmslow, Cheshire SK9 6AR, England.

British Library Cataloguing in Publication Data

A CIP catalogue record for this book is available from the British Library.

ISBN: 1-85058-526-1

Typesetting and design by

Sigma Press, Wilmslow

Printed in Malta by
Interprint Ltd.

Distributed by

John Wiley & Sons Ltd., Baffins Lane, Chichester, West Sussex, England.

NORTH EAST WORCS
COLLEGE
93816 R
~~005.75~~ 006.6

Acknowledgement of copyright names

Within this book, various proprietary trade names and names protected by copyright are mentioned for descriptive purposes. Full acknowledgment is hereby made of all such protection.

PREFACE

This practical book is aimed at users, producers, systems and software developers, educators, and virtually anyone that wants to know more about PC multimedia. It is a combination of technical information, theory and practice, current thinking, philosophy, a comprehensive glossary of acronyms and terms, and numerous contact listings. The latter is a sort of "Who's doing what in PC multimedia."

It should be said that, though some of the text may appear technical at first sight, the multimedia producer need not be a technically-minded individual. It is creative and artistic people that excel in multimedia. Closely linked to film, video, television and audio visual production, multimedia development is often considered outside the domain of many conventional computer professions. Thankfully not all computer professionals are 'conventional'.

I have written this book because of the amazing growth of what might be termed the PC multimedia marketplace. I also want to remind people of the enormous benefits and opportunities that PC multimedia continues to yield, as well as to inform them of recent advancements. One of the most significant of these has been the launch of affordable CD-R (CD-Recordable) drives such as the Philips CDD521. These have brought economical, low-volume CD-ROM (Compact Disc – Read Only Memory) replication to the desktop – desktop CD-ROM publishing is now a reality. The increase in data transfer rate of modern so-called dual-speed CD-ROM drives such as the NEC Intersect CDR74 and Apple CD300i is also significant, as is the launch of the quadspeed Pioneer DRM-604X, which is specified as producing a continuous 600Kbytes/sec.

Lastly, if you or your company is engaged in multimedia – or even Virtual Reality-related industries and you would like to be listed in the next edition of either Multimedia, CD-ROM & CD, please contact me c/o Sigma Press. I hope that this book proves both useful and enjoyable.

Francis Botto

For

Silke Rosema

&

Lydia Sunjerga

CONTENTS

1

Introduction

'Links and quotations stretchin g forever into the horizon, as if a great literature that will expand. I think I know how Descartes felt: the x and y stretching forever, dividing all mathematics, and realising that he was the first person to stand at the centre but it wasn't the centre, the centre itself could be.' – Ted Nelson

A product of the Multimedia PC Marketing Council Inc, the Multimedia PC (MPC) now represents one of the largest installed multimedia user bases and audiences. It is served by a richly diverse array of MPC titles, which range from inexpensive entertainment variants to useful encyclopedias like Microsoft's Encarta. Encarta (illustrated below) is one of a new breed of sophisticated *AYLI* (as-you-left-it) MPC titles, which reloads exactly as left when last used.

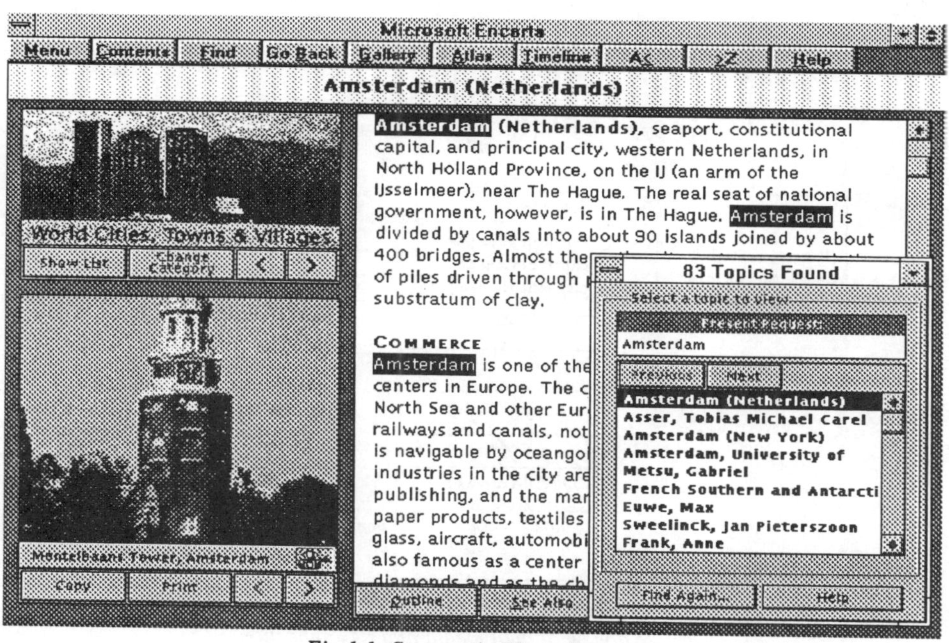

Fig 1.1: Screen-shot from Encarta

Also served by numerous different multimedia authoring tools, video recorders or video capture boards, advanced CD-ROM (Compact Disc – Read Only Memory) drives, and numerous sound cards, the PC is perhaps one of the most flexible and cost-effective multimedia development platforms. Low-budget multimedia productions can be implemented using little more than Microsoft Video for Windows (VfW) together with a video recorder, an appropriate authoring tool and a low-cost 8-bit sound card such as SoundBlaster Pro or one of the many others. Admittedly the end result may be a little basic, but will nonetheless suit many people's needs or pockets.

Numerous Windows video recorders such as VideoBlaster and VideoSpygot permit the creation of part-motion, part-screen video (PMPSV). Resultant video clips can be embedded into OLE (Object Linking and Embedding) compliant Windows applications in the form of objects.

You can create more advanced multimedia through the inclusion of (near) full-motion, full-screen video (FMFSV) using more sophisticated video recorders (or video capture boards) such as the Intel variants based on the i750 chipset. Digithurst and VideoLogic also produce video boards capable of recording and playing back FMFSV. Coupled with a 16-bit sound card, such an MPC authoring station presents the producer or developer with a most powerful medium in which to work. Used together with appropriate editing software FMFSV recorders need not be confined to multimedia. They are equally useful to the digital film-maker working with desktop video.

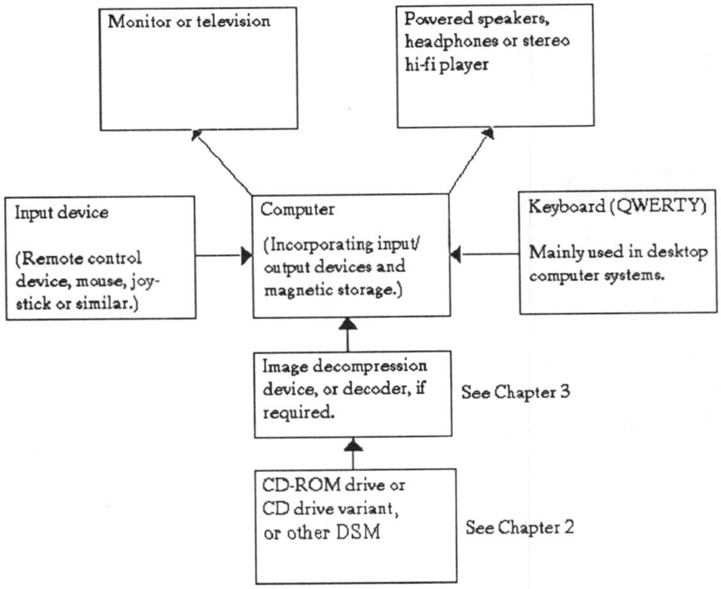

Fig 1.2: a view of multimedia and its connections

Through its many communications with the computer press, Microsoft once insisted that multimedia did not represent a market *per se*, but was a medium that would enrich a number of diverse products in different markets. While this is a fair assertion in terms of business software and perhaps games systems, it can be argued that multimedia appliances such as CDTV (Commodore Dynamic Total Vision), Philips CDI (Compact Disc Interactive), the Windows-based Tandy VIS (Video Information System) serve a new market for consumer multimedia systems. Equally, manufactures of Multimedia PCs (MPCs) and MPC peripheral devices serve other new markets.

That multimedia systems such as CDI players, CDTV, Tandy VIS, and the Sony MMCD are pitched at the consumer market, highlights the mass-market appeal of multimedia. It is this fact that makes multimedia as important a breakthrough as the commercial availability of the affordable desktop computer; it not only touches people at their place of work but in their homes, too. Both the Sony MMCD and Tandy VIS can be described loosely as PC multimedia systems.

Combining still and moving images, sound, audio, text and interactivity, multimedia has initially culminated in a re-evaluation of the ways in which we communicate information. Unlike linear, non-interactive media such as broadcast television, it can provide users with a choice of numerous meaningful paths. For example, select information about Albert Einstein and expect to be presented with such options as 'Theory of Relativity', 'Biography', 'Universe' and so forth. Interaction of this sort permits users to gain personal interpretations, or to reap essential facts only.

Day-to-day applications of multimedia can be visualised by considering activities that resemble the process of communicating information. Examples include education and training, reference, point-of-information, business presentations, manuals, corporate communications, simulations, databases, geographic information systems, advertising, documentaries and so on.

The term multimedia is yet broader than even these diverse applications suggest, and its usage will probably become vague, rather like the terms science or scientist. Through interactive games and leisure programs, a significant number of users may regard multimedia as home entertainment. Equally, computer users often see it as adding animation, video clips, voice-annotation and sound bites to software.

The underlying technology will also spawn offshoots, of which the most notable will be video-telecommunications and video-teleconferencing. With the growing popularity of video phones it will be but a short time before the widespread availability of plug-in cards that allow you to do the same on a desktop computer. Wrongly, these may also come under the heading of multimedia.

1.1 Technology

'It is imminent that multimedia will be superseded by VR – an infinitely more powerful medium and a mandatory inclusion in everyone's long-range continuum focusing on either Microsoft Windows or System 7. But there is a great deal of work to be done before VR becomes as practical and as accessible as multimedia. Before we can cross that long bridge to VR we need to climb the highest mountain ever climbed, and this is multimedia... It is not being climbed because it is there, it is being climbed because there is no way around it.' – Francis Michael

From the printed page to broadcast television, and from multimedia to virtual reality (VR), each successful new medium brings new professions, or at least brings changes to some of those that already exist. By accident or by design, more and more people now find themselves working in PC multimedia-related industries, serving some of the fastest growing markets in Europe, North America and Asia. So what is multimedia, technically, and what are its mechanics?

Defining multimedia technically is rather like saying that the combustion engine is a machine, which, through the ignition of fuel in a cylinder, provides a reciprocating piston movement that is converted into angular motion. The fact that it changed many aspects of everyday life is totally ignored.

Technically, multimedia can also be oversimplified. It represents the convergence between computers, digital video, digital audio and sound synthesis.

Distribution media for such material include Compact Disc – Read Only Memory (CD-ROM), Compact Disc Interactive (CDI), and CD-ROM XA (Extended Architecture) discs. Standard 12 cm diameter CD-ROM and CD-I discs typically support up to about 660 Mbytes data storage capacity.

Many are enthralled by the resultant eclectic mix, which yields interesting if not mind-boggling possibilities. We can combine still or motion video, animation, computer generated images, sound synthesis, audio, text and interactivity.

A stand-alone PC multimedia system (See Fig. 1.1) will almost always include the following components:

- Standard PC together with QWERTY keyboard, hard disk, Dram, graphics controller etc.
- Appropriate VGA (or better) display (television, CRT monitor or portable LCD or TFT display)
- User-interaction (or input device) such as a remote control device, mouse, joy-stick, touch screen, or

- User interface (UI) such as Windows 3.x/NT, Modular Windows, OS/2 Presentation Manager
- Operating System (OS) such as MS-DOS, DR-DOS, OS/2, or Unix;
- CD-ROM drive, which might be CD-ROM XA (eXtended Architecture) compliant (See Chapter 3);
- Sound card such as Turtle Beach MultiSound, SoundBlaster Pro, SoundBlaster 16 ASP, MediaVision Pro Audio Spectrum, Roland LAPC1, Ad Lib GOLD, or Microsoft Windows Sound System;
- Stereo amplifier with accompanying speakers, or self-powered speakers, or simply a pair of headphones.

Using a conventional (current) PC the delivery of FMFSV requires an appropriate decoder/decompressor. Such devices read compressed video, and decompress it while playing it back.

It is also possible to decompress digital video through software alone. Comparatively inexpensive to develop, software solutions can be assumed less effective regarding both picture size and attainable frame rate.

Some CD-ROM multimedia titles can be delivered using nothing more than a standard computer linked to a CD-ROM drive. A multimedia encyclopedia, for example, might combine audio, illustrations, animations and motion video clips. Typically, these will be PMPSV occupying around 25 percent of the screen and running between five and 15 frames per second (fps).

A multimedia system can also take the form of a standard computer such as PC connected to a videodisc player. A system example is an IBM PS/2 fitted with an IBM M-Motion Video Adapter/A. This can be used to extract, digitise and display analogue video emanating from videodisc or other source.

Videodisc players are very much part of Interactive Video (IV). Now a mature technology, this illustrated the potential of motion video in a computer environment. However, the storage of analogue video has now reached a plateau beyond which it will not progress because attention has rightly switched to digital video.

1.2 Multimedia Applications

Certain mainstream multimedia applications are used daily by a growing number of people, for example:

- The education sector, for instance, is embracing the collective technology for presentations, computer-aided learning (CAL) and reference.

- In the corporate and industrial sectors, multimedia is used extensively for training and business presentations. Renault, for example, use a multimedia program called 'Ediris' for training car mechanics.
- Retailers and consumers are benefiting from in-store point-of-sale (POS) and point-of-information (POI) terminals. Both approaches are proven to increase customer spending.
- Multimedia is more and more widely used as a publishing medium, with many of the leading publishers including Dorling Kindersley, Oxford University Press, Longman and Harper Collins playing active roles.

Though most publishers have been remarkably slow to respond to multimedia, many are now moving from basic paper and electronic publishing into the arena of multimedia. Often the resultant titles are collaborative ventures between book publishers and software houses or traditional record companies that have become multimedia producers. For example, Microsoft Musical Instruments was produced using intellectual property provided by Dorling Kindersley Ltd. In a similar vein, Harper-Collins works closely with Nimbus Information Systems. And like Nimbus, once a traditional record company, Chrysalis has spread its wings through the emergence of Chrysalis Multi Media Ltd.

The nature of multimedia means that almost all commercial titles have to be collaborative ventures involving publishers, record companies and software houses. Microsoft Multimedia Beethoven, for example, incorporates recordings owned by Decca Record Company (London).

Other than entertainment titles, multimedia applications share the common function of communicating information. The following subsections discuss some of these, highlighting comparative advantages and what can be expected from them today and in the future.

1.2.1 Education

'The need to improve the quality of education both in the home and school environment will be one of the most universal priorities in society during the next decade... a truly multimedia system can offer the type of breakthrough required...'

G.A.J Bastiaens & G. Stulberg

Multimedia is widely acknowledged as an environment with great potential in education. It is able to assist both the pupil/student and teacher/lecturer in new ways. For the teacher or lecturer it provides a means of putting across information and ideas, and for the pupil or student it can represent a one-to-one teaching environment which moves at the required pace.

An early pilot program for the Intel platform (for multimedia on IBM and compatible machines) was Palenque, developed with the assistance of Bank Street College of

Education New York. This courseware facilitates the exploration of an ancient Mayan site, giving access to a multimedia database containing audio-visual experiences. Through a joint venture with Shell, Philips also produced an early educational program for its multimedia platform (CDI). The disc, by SPIN UK, seeks to make mathematics and science more engaging.

At its simplest level, multimedia is harnessed as a presentation tool with which only the teacher or lecturer interacts. Material might represent a pictorial and textual presentation used to enhance a lesson or lecture. In some instances this might be intended as a complete lesson or lecture for dialogue between student/pupil and system, but shortage of systems/terminals restricts this mode of operation.

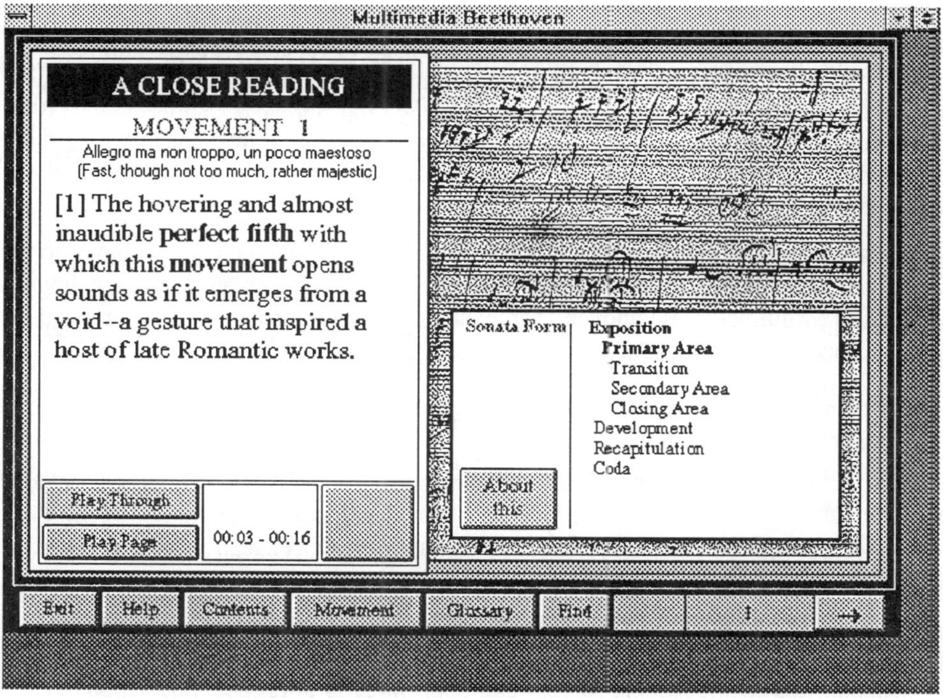

Fig 1.3: Sound and vision enhance the 'Beethoven' CD-ROM

The true power of multimedia manifests itself through pupil/student interaction, thus leaving the teacher/lecturer to oversee events and to answer queries. In this guise, multimedia can act like a teacher or lecturer constantly available with expert tuition.

That pupils/students should interact with multimedia is a key aspect of its role in education. An Intel paper on Digital Video Interactive (DVI) states that interactive multimedia can yield as much as 70 percent recall, as opposed to 45 percent for audio-visual aids, and just 25 percent for audio. Many CAL experts are undecided as to the precise improvement such interaction gives. That there is an improvement, however, is agreed.

Distribution of multimedia lessons, lectures and courseware on CD-ROM or CDI disc adds another dimension to multimedia in education, providing a vehicle for pupils/students to take lessons/lectures at home. For scattered rural communities where schools are inaccessible, and for institutes running distance learning (or correspondence) courses of any kind, the potential is enormous. Indeed a portion of courses run by institutions that depend upon home learning (e.g. The Open University and The Open College) will certainly be distributed through multimedia in future (See Chapter 2). Affordable consumer systems such as CDI players and the Commodore Dynamic Total Vision (CDTV) closely resemble the sort of systems that could provide a basis for this (See Chapter 3).

It is important to note that multimedia is not poised to replace teachers and lecturers overnight (See Chapter 5). In addition to current technical constraints, technology is expensive and therefore inaccessible for many educational establishments. With adequate long-term support, however, it will certainly alter the generally accepted study methods of the pupil/student, while transforming traditional teaching methods along the way.

1.2.2 Training

Ranging from simple induction courses to sales techniques, corporate and industry training has in recent years become ever-more dependent upon technology. Computer-based training (CBT) now forms a substantial market. Indeed education and training are the fastest growing markets for multimedia products.

Training requirements often differ from one company to the next and are seldom satisfied through off-the-shelf products. The development of in-house training material is therefore common. This is different from the education sector, where a higher level of standardisation exists.

Multimedia represents a powerful solution to training, where employees can interact with video under computer control. Many commercially available authoring systems lend themselves particularly well to the development of CBT courseware. Obtaining the most out of these usually demands programming with general purpose languages such as C (See Glossary). Programming is easier where the package includes commonly used library routines.

Such systems must be capable of controlling a videodisc player, should be easy to use, and offer a variety of library routines. Popular authoring systems that fit this profile include TenCORE, TopClass, Authorware Professional, Quest and IBM's Audio Visual Connection (AVC).

Advantages of multimedia in education also apply to corporate and industry training. And because places of work often operate on a 24-hour basis, it can offer the added advantage of constant availability.

1.2.3 Point-of-information

Traditionally, consumer education has consisted of publishing product brochures, advertising, allowing the potential customer to peruse in a shop or showroom, and product demonstrations.

These generally accepted ways in which the consumer chooses an appropriate product can be aided or replaced using multimedia in a point-of-information (POI) guise. POI terminals present the customer with the ability to browse through product ranges, or experience just those items that fit a user-defined profile.

POI can be a powerful marketing and advertising tool providing the means to display products. The benefits are clear: it gives an opportunity to promote products in a medium that cannot be rivalled by (current) television advertising. It also allows small and medium-sized companies to promote products on terms that only large companies and corporations could previously afford.

Furthermore, if products can be demonstrated adequately through multimedia, the need to exhibit them physically becomes unnecessary and so floor space can be saved. Research also indicates that users of POI terminals spend more money than those shoppers using conventional means. Finally, the possibility of fewer sales staff is raised.

With the growing number of multimedia systems in the home and with the falling price of disc replication, we may well see POI distributed free like 'junk mail'. In the computer industry, there is also the possibility of distributing short advertisements/ demonstrations containing video sequences on floppy disk. Transmitting such multimedia directly into the home is also a distinct possibility and is one that is being researched and developed by several US companies.

Multimedia can also help the consumer in making general decisions. Computer graphics, combined with video texturing, can help users decide on a colour scheme for the home, for instance. 'Design and Decorate' co-developed by Intel and Videodisc Publishing, Inc., New York, shows how multimedia technology can be used for interior design. This permits the user to design a living room, choosing everything from the shape and size of room, to furnishing and accessories.

Museums of various kinds throughout the world have installed POI terminals. These give visitors the opportunity to follow user-defined guided tours. Such an approach also allows visitors to experience interesting items which might otherwise be catalogued and hidden away from public view. Many other areas such as careers advice, geographic information systems, surrogate travel (brochures) are also possible through POI.

1.2.4 User-interfaces

It is agreed that computers are generally difficult to use because of the awkward means through which user-interaction takes place. Many users remain enslaved to the QWERTY keyboard, having to enter numerous keyboard commands.

With the introduction of the Macintosh computer, Apple showed that a Graphical User Interface (GUI) and a mouse provided a friendlier interactive environment. Showing icons and menu items that lead to various applications and features, a GUI simply requires the user to point and click a mouse.

Following its commercial success, the GUI concept was made available for all professional personal computers. It can now be seen on the IBM PC, IBM PS/2, Atari ST, Commodore Amiga, workstations and other machines.

The PC fraternity was initially given the 'Gem' visual interface. This shields the user from Disk Operating System (DOS) keyboard commands. For instance, using DOS to run a program called Paradox in the pdox4 directory, it is necessary (using DOS) to enter cd\pdox4 followed by Paradox. Gem merely requires the user to point and click on an icon representing the pdox4 directory and then click on an icon for the paradox program. Today, Microsoft Windows and Presentation Manager represent two popular GUIs for the IBM PC and compatible machines.

At the simplest level, multimedia can enhance the GUI concept by transforming icons into motion icons (micons). Invented by the Norwegian Hans Peter Brondmo at Massachusetts Institute of Technology (MIT) in 1989, micons consist of a series of frames that are run in a continuous loop. For example, an option on the screen that leads to a flat file database might be represented by a person flicking through a card box. As with icons, micons are often reinforced with concise descriptions.

Micons manifest more clearly the information, features or applications to which screen options are tagged. It is reasonable to assume that they will consolidate with the current (commercial) user-interface approach, coexisting for some time with the generally-accepted 'buttons' and 'icons'.

The pace at which micons will proliferate through business software such as relational databases, word processors and spreadsheets, is likely to be gradual for two reasons. Firstly, when parallels are drawn with icons, few business programs had incorporated these some five years after their commercial introduction. Secondly, business software is traditionally functional with bland screens.

Multimedia can have a greater impact on UIs than the mere introduction of micons. For example, speech synthesis and audio is now used to reinforce menu selections, thus reducing time spent making choices visually. Voice mail, where telephone messages can be stored away on your PC, and voice-annotation of Windows where sound bites are attached to various basic operations, has become common.

1.2.5 Software training

The continual introduction of Information Technology, and its pace of change, give rise to a thriving software training industry. This bears testimony to the fact that current commercial software and computers are simply too difficult to use.

Evidence of this is seen when a new program is introduced into an office environment: the need for training or retraining emerges instantly. Equally, new employees often have to be trained to use word processors, databases, spreadsheets, integrated packages and so forth.

Depending upon product sophistication, training normally consists of a one- to three-day course, the overall cost of which can be considerable. However, initial high training costs drop off significantly for all but those companies with a high turnover of staff.

There is, however, a feasible and cost-effective multimedia solution to software training as well as to program documentation. The program and documentation could be distributed on a single CD-ROM disc. An installation program (on CD-ROM) can be used to write the program to hard disk, thus accommodating system configuration, various options chosen, and the type of printer installed.

Multimedia manuals and training material could both be loaded from CD-ROM. A movable and re-sizable window could be used to accommodate such material. The window could even be switched off leaving just verbal instructions. More than this, the text-based, context-sensitive help systems of today could be transformed into motion video and dialogue. Theoretically, then, multimedia could radically alter software training and documentation.

1.3 Home Multimedia

Consumer systems such as CDI players and CDTV (See Chapter 3) give home users the ability to play multimedia distributed on either CDI or CD-ROM discs. Entertainment through interactive games and leisure programs is a popular application of such systems.

The widespread installation of PCs in the home points to a bright future for computer-based multimedia systems. Multimedia technology has the potential to transform the personal computer into a universal 'home system', adding to the list of current popular applications:

Video player (digital video storage techniques enable computers to play movies, offering superior sound quality to VHS). DVI (Digital Video Interactive) implemented with the Intel 750 chipset, was originally developed for this purpose;

Multimedia;

Television;

Video-telecommunications (See Section 1.4);

Video-teleconferencing;

E-mail (See Glossary);

Communications;

Electronic news services/newspapers;

Mainstream computing and specialist computer applications;

Audio CD player;

CD-ROM reader;

Home working;

Viewing PhotoCDs (See Chapter 2).

There is a real prospect of a 'home system' that could embody a significant portion of consumer electronics devices as well as be a communications device and computer. Evidently, computer technology will exist in symbiosis with consumer electronics, where the increasingly fine line that separates the two will become yet finer.

1.4 Communications

Multimedia technology will yield more than 'multimedia', causing us to re-evaluate the role of the computer. For example, through developments in digital video and particularly real-time video compression, video-telecommunications using personal computers is well on its way to commercial availability. If cost should rule out video capture and delivery at 30 frames per second (fps), a more economical 10 fps, or even less, will suffice.

Video-teleconferencing is another associated application with immense potential. To appreciate what this means, imagine using a computer and you wish to communicate with a colleague. Video-teleconferencing would allow you to see your colleague in a window on your monitor screen and *vice-versa*, allowing you both to talk face to face as if round a table. Such technology leads to more efficient use of personnel and in the longer term, could open the door to a far-flung workforce. In mid-1991, ICL announced a desktop conferencing system that runs under Microsoft Windows. Users are able to write to the screen using a special stylus.

1.5 Hypertext

Just as modern multimedia led to a re-evaluation of the way we communicate information in the eighties and nineties, hypertext had a similar impact in the sixties. Interestingly, the birth of what is now known as hypertext can be traced back to the 1940s (See Chapter 5).

The rationale behind the development of hypertext was a simple one: to optimise the processes of writing, storing textual information, and accessing that information. Hypertext improves accessibility of stored information by eliminating the need to follow rigourous set sequences. It allows the user to reference masses of related material through the pursuit of *ad hoc* paths. Advantages of this are easily understood when considering traditional methods. A word unknown to the reader of a book first leads to the index being searched. Failing this, the reader naturally attempts to find reference to the word in another book. The many references required to research a subject or satisfy curiosity is time-consuming.

With information linked, indexed and stored on computer, hypertext expedites this process, and gives users the opportunity to take regular excursions to satisfy references. It also makes information available that would not otherwise occur to the casual reader. The word car, for instance, might be linked to numerous options such as: combustion engine, Henry J. Ford, Detroit, Rolls-Royce, Catalytic Convertor, and a whole host of relevant texts.

Though hypertext is a superior method of imparting information, it is not without disadvantages, and these are raised in Chapter 5. Hypertext is equally useful when writing or simply arranging gathered information. An appropriate hypertext tool, such as BrainStorm, can be used to implant and manifest links between related items of text automatically. For example, consider drafting an outline using a hypertext tool and beginning with top-level items (or chapter headings):

- Multimedia Introduction
- CD-ROM
- Multimedia Systems
- Hypertext
- Hypermedia

Expanding the first heading, the following development might take place:

- Multimedia Introduction
- CD-ROM
- CD-ROM disc
- Capacity
- Modes A and B
- CD-ROM
- Multimedia Systems
- Hypertext
- Hypermedia

In this example, CD-ROM is linked to its 'namesake', thus allowing items listed under the section CD-ROM to be made available through the chapter heading CD-ROM; by moving the cursor to the chapter heading CD-ROM, you would also be presented with items listed under the section heading CD-ROM. Such hypertext tools offer a powerful means of outlining, conventional program design, and hypertext material design. (Using hypertext word processors, links can be implanted between different files.)

To the conventional writer, hypertext can eliminate the possibility of duplication and assist in the development of rigourous structures. Program design is optimised by manifesting certain procedures or subroutines that will be run more than once during program execution. This approach lends itself to structured programming and to object orientated programming (OOP).

To the developer of hypertext material, such tools can prove invaluable, as vital links are implanted. The many links that logically unite the information to be presented, are also highlighted.

However simple the concept may appear, hypertext cannot be underestimated as it is an important component of multimedia. The terms multimedia and hypertext are often inseparable, and in the early days, many wrongly considered them to be interchangeable (See Chapter 5).

1.6 Hypermedia

Hypermedia consists of hypertext combined with still or moving images and sound. Unfortunately, 'hypermedia' and 'hypertext' are two more terms that may be wrongly interchanged. Strictly speaking, hypertext relies on text only.

Available to Macintosh users through HyperCard since 1987, hypermedia is a relatively mature area of multimedia. HyperCard for the Apple Macintosh can be considered as the earliest commercially successful hypermedia authoring tool that combined text, graphics, animated sequences and sound. It made the Macintosh an effective personal computer for multimedia. A plethora of hypermedia authoring tools has since emerged, including ToolBook for the Microsoft Windows environment on the IBM PC and compatible machines. Hypermedia applications developed using such tools can be thought of as interactive books that combine images, text and sound.

1.7 News Media

Electronic newspapers will have a marked effect on the sale of traditional daily broadsheets. In the United Kingdom, the slow decline of newspaper sales seen in the early nineties was considered by many as a result of the recession. While this is a reasonable assertion, the more widespread availability and use of electronic news services at this time must also have played a part in placing downward pressure on circulations.

When Rupert Murdoch of News Corporation slashed the price of *The Times* (London) in 1993, it was disclosed that this was intended to reverse the circulation decline. Competing newspapers saw it as an act of aggression, with one paper's editor claiming that it was intended to put them out of business. To coincide with this price reduction, Murdoch bought Delphi Internet Services, an electronic newspaper developer. Irrespective of the rationale behind Murdoch's price cuts of this time, it spelled the beginning of a new era in newspaper publishing.

1.7.1 Electronic newspapers

Reading a newspaper is an inefficient way of absorbing information. Headlines help, but these are arranged according to editors' judgement, with which your interests may fail to coincide. As a result, the information that you need might be hidden away at the bottom of a page or not included at all. We could resort to cynicism here and place about as much faith in news editors as the tutor Samuel Johnson once quoted, placed in his students: 'Read over your compositions, and where ever you meet with a passage which you think is particularly fine, strike it out.'

Electronic news services are a great improvement over broadsheets. Whether we rely on newspapers, radio or television, there is a price to be paid for linear, non-interactive media. The reader/listener/viewer is tied to a fixed sequence of events and just one viewpoint on each story or feature.

Achieving an unbiased view of current affairs requires that you read more than one newspaper, listen to more than one radio station, and watch more than one television channel. This is unpractical. Evidently news in general, and more importantly the way in which we receive it, is unsatisfactory. To many, the Herculean task of solving these problems completely is something of a Utopian ideal. However, the inefficiency of reading vast amounts of text to uncover a few relevant facts could be optimised by making more information available through electronic means. For example, with appropriate indexing and linking (using hypertext or hypermedia), the reader could access information on CD-ROM disc instantly.

CD-ROM is already used to distribute the annual contents of some magazines and newspapers. Also, there are several pilot schemes publishing interactive magazines on CD-ROM. It is at this point, however, that we have to dispense with CD variants in their current form, and look toward the global network. Clearly, the real solution lies in a global electronic depository of all news and information (See Chapter 5).

The problem of achieving an unbiased view is probably the most complex and most difficult to solve. Of course, the assumption that people want such a view of news and current affairs might be misguided.

It is not unrealistic to predict that one day it will be feasible to receive personalised newspapers. With an appropriately linked computer in the home, it will be possible to receive reports from different news agencies, publications and publishers. Beyond this, it is reasonable to forecast the emergence of multimedia news broadcasting. (Interactive television news already exists in the US.) It could be said that one day you will even be able to program a system to receive the exact 'multimedia television news programme' required.

However, such personalised news could fuel a sort of tunnel vision, as the recipient will usually list only the things that he or she believes to want to see or read. Linear media have their faults but they can provide reasonably balanced views. For example, the documentary, book or feature that would have been omitted from a personalised publication or programme, often turns out to be quite interesting when given a chance.

1.8 Origins

'As a hobby, the eighties were about as interesting as chest pains... It was only when the slouches started waking up to multimedia and virtual reality in the late eighties and early nineties did I awake. Multimedia had reached critical mass, so giving people like me something to do other than write for boring computer magazines... I mean people stopped looking at you as if you were completely crazy the minute your uttered a sentence about either multimedia or VR. Imagine, the so-called 'sane' people were talking about the same things as us – well almost.' Francis Michael

The origins of multimedia are frequently connected with the emergence of the term 'hypertext', and with an earlier means of information storage and retrieval devised in the forties (See Chapter 5). These represent the most notable milestones until the late eighties, when the technology for truly interactive multimedia emerged. The term 'multimedia' was first used in the Sixties to describe simple tape-and-slide presentations.

Beginning with optical storage, the first breakthrough was Philips LaserVision, a videodisc system capable of storing still video, motion video and audio data (each in analogue form). Launched in 1978 (and Europe in 1982) as a consumer product for playing video films, LaserVision quickly led to IV. This yielded the first taste of video in a computer environment.

The real significance of LaserVision was that it provided a basis for the development of the Compact Disc – Digital Audio (CD-DA) (1982), which in turn led to the announcement of CD-ROM, and later to CD-I. Philips issued the first provisional CDI specification in June 1986 (See Chapter 3), making it commercially available for the consumer in 1991 (US) and 1992 (Europe).

1986 also saw the launch of CUBIC-CT by Creative Labs, Inc (Santa Clara). This system delivered music, had a voice input and output, enhanced graphics and used an electronic mass storage device. It was not a success, and Creative Labs now attribute its commercial failure to a lack of software, but CUBIC-CT was the world's first digital multimedia system.

In July 1987 Compact Disc – Video (CD-V) was launched. This provides a means of storing digital audio and digital video. In response to CDI, Intel made available an equivalent technology for the PC. Called DVI it was initially demonstrated by RCA and General Electric at the Microsoft CD-ROM conference of 1987. (DVI was originally pioneered for video distribution.) The DVI chip set was accommodated on two boards in 1990 and 1991, one for motion video delivery and another for video and audio capture.

Philips' response to DVI was to instigate the development of CD-ROM XA (Extended Architecture). Like DVI this was initially intended to open up the PC market. Announced by Philips, Sony and Microsoft in August 1988, it currently permits (near) CDI delivery in the PC environment. It is important to note that CD-ROM XA is not 100 percent downward compatible with CDI (See Chapter 3).

Microcomputer graphics was technically immature for much of the eighties. The Apple Lisa computer supported colour graphics but, like all other machines of the early eighties it was slow and limited regarding pixel resolution and numbers of colours. More powerful computer graphics systems such as the Cromenco SDI existed but were prohibitively expensive.

PC computer graphics matured as late as mid-1987 when IBM released the Video Graphics Array (VGA) standard, which embodied an analogue monitor port. Initially launched as part of the Personal System/2 (PS/2) range, it raised the standing of PC computer graphics.

The Macintosh included an analogue monitor port approximately three years before the PC, earlier; and in 1987 Apple launched HyperCard, the most successful and best-known microcomputer hypermedia product.

Historically, the collective technology we now call digital multimedia was first realised by Creative Labs in 1986 with CUBIC-CT, and HyperCard became the first major hypermedia product from a leading producer. But in terms of the consumer market, multimedia technology came of age in April 1991 (US and Europe) with the launch of the Commodore CDTV.

2

CD-ROM

"Today, in software, print publishing, and entertainment companies large and small around the world, growing numbers of talented people are working hard to develop the great CD-ROM products that will fulfil the immense potential of this medium. To accomplish this, we need to develop a common language, and we need to better understand what each of our points of view has to offer. We need mechanisms for resolving issues, and we need procedures for cooperative ventures. We've made great progress toward these goals since 1984, but we've also raised our expectations of what is possible. For as much as we've accomplished, the need for better understanding of common issues has never been greater..... I am excited by the quality and vision of the work now underway on CD-ROM products throughout the industry. I believe more than ever that CD-ROM products will be a major force in the expansion of the information industry, extending the benefits of personal computing to a much wider market." Bill Gates

With its comparatively large data storage capacity, CD-ROM (Compact Disc-Read Only Memory) is a standard component of the MPC specification. In fact it is CD-ROM that made possible the idea of sophisticated multimedia in the PC environment.

Since the earlier drives, which were based on the audio CD standard operation and architecture, significant advancements have been made in terms of the data transfer rates attainable. The original data transfer rates of 150 Kbytes/sec have been doubled by so-called 'double-spin' drives. In fact 1992 saw the commercial availability of quad-speed drives capable of sustaining around 600 Kbytes/sec. Mass storage devices have long-since been established as an important resource to make available electronic data on the PC. The advent of CD-ROM marked the beginning of a new era during which the emphasis is likely to switch from magnetic storage to optical technology.

Rewritable magnetic media such as floppy disk, hard disk and tape are familiar to almost all users of technology. Both removable and compact, floppy disk provides a vehicle for distributing programs and data. The often non-removable hard disk supports random access for large amounts of data, typically starting at around a meagre 20 Mbytes. Disk drives supporting hundreds of Mbytes are proliferating, and drives in the Giga byte (1,024 Mbytes) range are commercially available.

Magnetic tape provides a cost-effective means of storing large amounts of data where random-access is not required. For example, data back-up, archive purposes, and for submission of CD-ROM data to replication companies (See Chapter 5). Used to back up hard disks, *tape streamers* offer a safety net in the event of a catastrophic system failure. Subsequent data recovery simply involves reading the tape contents back to a functioning hard disk.

A read-only digital storage medium (DSM), CD-ROM supports up to about 660 Mbytes data storage capacity in standard form (See Section 2.4.1). It offers numerous features unrivalled by current magnetic media, including vast storage capacity, compactness of design, reliability and durability. Attributes such as these make CD-ROM ideal for the distribution of computer software, courseware, maps, databases, reference material, multimedia and more. In publishing it is particularly appropriate for annual releases of magazines and newspapers, providing random access to thousands of indexed articles, columns and reviews. The growing CD-ROM user base will result in less specialised publications and it is reasonable to assume that low-cost books and magazines/journals will appear in significant numbers in the foreseeable future (See Section 2.2.2).

CD-ROM drives and magnetic storage devices began to coexist to a noticeable degree in 1985. The world-wide installed CD-ROM user base grew from 25,000 in 1986 to almost 400,000 in 1989 (See Fig. 2.1). This is rather disappointing when the comparative advantages of the technology are evaluated. However, rate of growth will accelerate in coming years, and many millions of CD-ROM users are envisaged by the mid nineties.

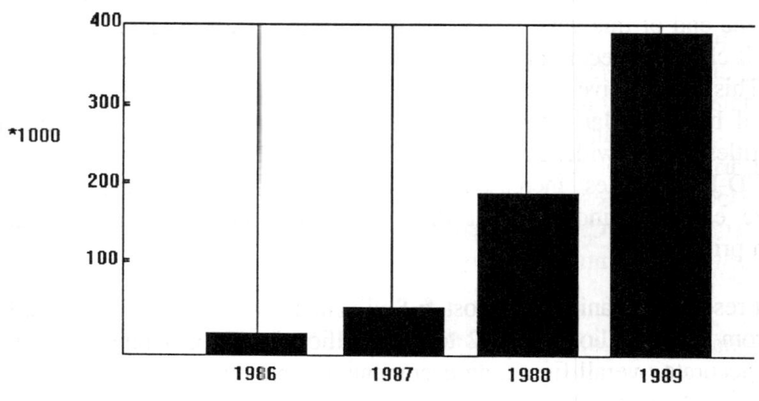

Fig 2.1

Growth in the CD-ROM user base will naturally provide the necessary momentum to make publishing on CD-ROM more viable, thus increasing numbers of commercial titles. Commercial titles available world-wide rose from around 100 in 1986 to about 900 in 1989, and to about 1,600 in 1990 (See Fig. 2.2). It is reasonable to assume that merits of CD-ROM technology indicate a brighter future where a saturation point is inconceivable in the nineties. The single influential factor in deciding the future of CD-ROM is the emergence or non-emergence of an equally standardised medium.

The cost of CD-ROM drives halved during the period 1985 to 1990 in the UK, where 1990 saw high specification drives priced at around £500. 1991 saw a further drop in price to around £400. In 1993, Mitsumi drives appeared in the direct channel, priced at less than £150.

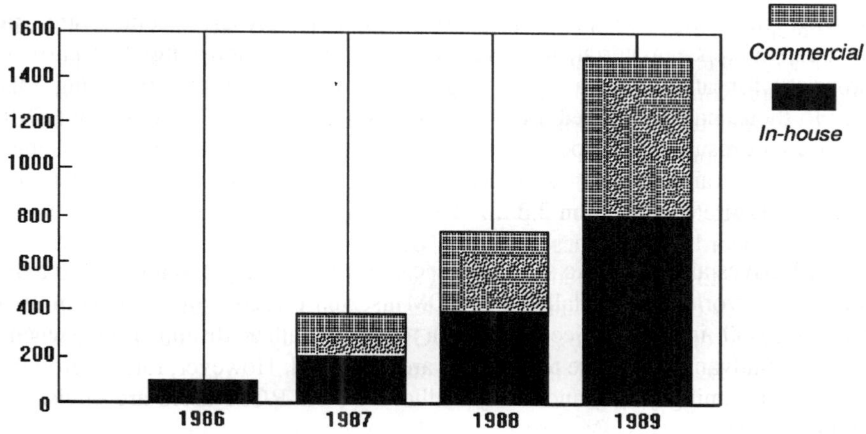

Fig 2.2

With the European installed CD-ROM drive base likely to reach more than 6.7 million by the end of this year, CD-ROM is about to realise the sort of critical mass that brings it closer to becoming, among other things, a *de facto* software distribution medium. This impressive 78% growth on the 1992 installed drive base is accompanied by a similarly favourable increase in both in-house and commercial CD-ROM titles, world-wide. From 1987 to 1989 numbers of both commercial and in-house CD-ROM titles increased consistently by 100%, annually, but now conservative estimates indicate that there may be over 5,000 commercial titles currently in print.

The market research organisation, Frost & Sullivan, estimates that CD sales in Europe will rise from $255 million in 1992 to $1.2 billion in 1996. While this may be a reasonably accurate overall figure, an accompanying pie chart that addresses sales of CDI (Interactive), CD-ROM, PhotoCD (See Section 2.2.5) and CD-ROM XA (eXtended Architecture) remains an area of contention.

Estimates of in-house titles vary dramatically largely because of the falling price of CD-R (Recordable) drives (See Section 2.9) such as the Philips CDD 521 which brings CD-ROM replication to the desktop when it comes to low volume runs, which are often below 50 (1993). The falling cost of such replication has led to a dramatic increase in the number of small and medium size companies taking advantage of CD-ROM for archiving purpose. The falling price of CD-R is one of a number of kickstarts CD-ROM has had over the past three years or so. Significance can be attached to the Microsoft Multimedia PC initiative as well as PhotoCD, which forms a key component of a $3.5 trillion market by 2001 that is to embody computers, consumer electronics, media, publishing and telecommunications.

2.1 CD-ROM

The standard 12cm diameter CD-ROM supports up to about 660 Mbytes (692,060,000 bytes) data capacity (See Section 2.4). A single disc is equivalent to between approximately 400 1.44 Mbyte floppy disks or 1,500 360 Kbyte floppy disks. 8cm diameter CD-ROMs exist, but are not cost effective for the moment due to the lack of an appropriate standard.

A 12cm CD-ROM can store up to 250,000 A4 pages of text or approximately 100,000,000 words. Note, these methods of quoting data capacity are rather vague and not likely to satisfy many people (See Section 2.4). Technically, using CD technology, data capacities many times greater than this can be achieved with little difficulty. Quad density drives giving 2.4 Gbytes already exist, but their proliferation is hindered by the absence of an adequate standard.

Like audio CD, a CD-ROM disc physically consists of a metallic disc bonded to a polycarbonate base. This is coated with a transparent, protective lacquer (See Fig. 2.3). A track spiralling from its centre measures some three miles long, and is arranged at a density of 16,000 tracks per inch.

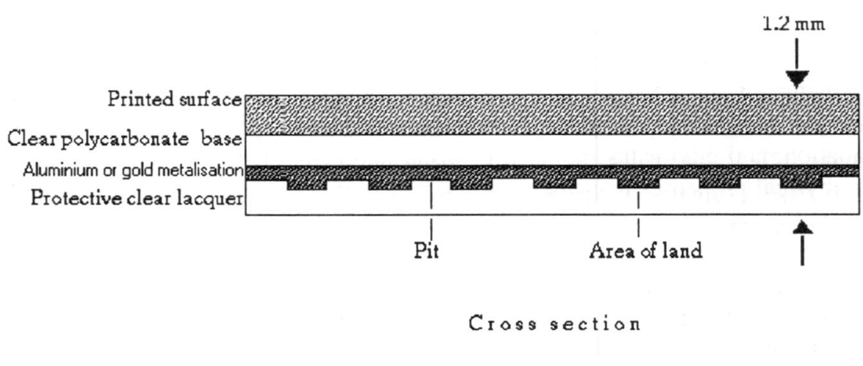

Fig 2.3

2.2 Applications

The emergence of CD-ROM highlights more clearly the many problems that exist when floppy disk is used as a distribution medium. Using current standard technology, a maximum of 1.44 Mbytes can be reaped from a single, standard floppy disk, whereas a standard CD-ROM yields around 400 times this. A mere 10 Mbytes of data requires nine 1.2 Mbyte disks, or eight 1.44 Mbyte disks, or 28 360 Kbyte disks. Currently, the 5.25'' 360 Kbyte disk is the most least effective commonly used medium for distribution purposes. On rare occasions 5.25'' floppy disks are prone to physical damage. Data corruption through the presence of electromagnetic fields is also a threat to magnetic media.

Equating to approximately 1,400 360 Kbyte floppy disks in standard form, CD-ROM epitomises compactness of design. It is reliable, virtually immune to physical damage, and impervious to data corruption through the presence of electromagnetic fields.

CD-ROM has potential to become a universal distribution medium used for everything from computer software to multimedia.

2.2.1 Computer Software Distribution

The first commercial CD-ROM software distribution disc from a major producer was Microsoft Office. Farallon Computing released lesser known programs on CD-ROM prior to this, as did Microsoft itself. Also PC Sig released the world's first shareware compilation on CD-ROM in the US.

With programs becoming increasingly complex due to demands imposed by advancements in software design and hardware, an ever-increasing number of floppy disks are required for distribution purposes. In the light of this and the growing CD-ROM user base, CD-ROM represents a more and more practical alternative.

Cost effectiveness of using CD-ROM naturally hinges upon the number of floppy disks (ie size of program and related data), and scale of distribution. However, CD-ROM need not be chosen purely for reasons of economy, because its basic convenience will often justify higher distribution costs. This basic convenience emanates from the fact that it helps smooth over the often tedious process of software installation, and eliminates the need to insert and re-insert floppy disks. In addition, their physical properties dispense with the return of corrupt or damaged floppy disks, benefiting users and vendors alike. Its most significant advantage is that of vast data storage capacity, of which the most sophisticated of current commercial programs would consume but a small portion. Spare storage space remaining can be used for program demonstrations. Eventually program documentation, training material and advertising could also be accommodated (See Chapter 1).

Many leading software producers could distribute their entire range of programs on a single CD-ROM. An increasing number of vendors will certainly do this in future when users will be assigned individual passwords for programs purchased. This can be achieved using one of a number of encryption methods. To read the encrypted CD-ROM an appropriate program with a unique password (serial number) can be distributed on floppy disk. Encryption can help prevent unauthorised access to CD-ROM data of all kinds.

Using (conventional) data compression methods, a single CD-ROM can yield more than a Gigabyte of programs and data. Phethean's PD Library, for instance, comprises around one Gigabyte of programs on a single disc.

Effects of CD-ROM as a distribution medium go beyond the mere replacement of floppy disk. Storage devices have a marked effect on the sophistication of commercial programs available. For example, not too long ago when hard disks were far from common, word processors were simple enough to be stored on a single 360 Kbyte floppy disk.

The need to archive program, data and text files is often unnecessary using CD-ROM. No longer will vendors be conscious of the meagre 100 Kbytes or so that a few text screens may consume. As drives and the related technology advance, increased rates of data transfer between drive and computer might mean that program files will eventually reside on CD-ROM. However, when swapping between applications stored on different discs we are faced with a problem, one solution to which lies is using magazine drives, daisy-chained drives or a CD-ROM network (See Section 2.7).

Alternatively, larger disc data storage capacities will emerge, in which case it might be advantageous for software producers to join forces and store programs on common discs. For example, one day you might be able to unlock Borland Paradox and WordPerfect from the same disc.

All things considered, software distribution via CD-ROM will become widespread, but floppy disk will not be cast into oblivion overnight like the vinyl disc in the music industry. Its basic convenience for backing up programs and data will ensure its existence for some time.

2.2.2 CD-ROM as a Publishing Medium

"The Encyclopedia Britannica could be reduced to the volume of a matchbox. The library of millions of volumes could be compressed into one end of a desk..."
Vannevar Bush

In retrospect, the belief that information technology would lead to the paperless office in the eighties is embarrassing when we consider that it led to even greater consumption of paper. It is now clear that optical storage techniques will be highly influential in moulding the paperless office. Rewritable optical storage devices lay at the heart of electronic filing systems such as Canon's Canofile, a desktop electronic filing system.

With CD-ROM we are now faced with the equally debatable prospect of a 'paperless library'. Like the paperless office it will surely emerge, but CD-ROM might not provide the key to this.

CD-ROM is a great deal more than a substitute for paper. Hypertext retrieval systems allow users to exploit textual information more fully. At a more basic level, greater flexibility than paper is achieved through indexing, where information can be accessed randomly and instantly. However, CD-ROM is not without disadvantages. Many users are unable to read from domestic television screens (using CDTV, for instance) for more than an hour or so. Some comfort is gained from the fact that the majority of CD-ROM drives are installed in systems connected to monitors. Although, these cannot always be taken as a significant improvement, because they fail to emulate paper sufficiently well. High specification computer monitors offer one solution, but these are far from widespread for reasons of cost.

However, the comparatively poor domestic television of today is likely to be superseded by high definition television (HDTV). The first impact of this will be on multimedia and interactive video systems.

Portability is an important prerequisite for any medium which is to take over from paper. An affordable book-sized CD-ROM reader simply has to materialise. More than just affordable, it has to be reasonably sophisticated and incorporate an appropriately sized display which is both sharp and fast.

In Japan, both Sanyo and Sony have launched portable CD-ROM readers which initially failed to interest in significant numbers even the Japanese consumer, the most demanding and responsive in the world. However, in more recent times Sony has achieved significant world-wide success through its Data Discman, which uses miniature CDs encoded according to the read-only Electronic Book (EB) format. Each disc can store up to 100,000 pages of text or 32,000 monochrome images. Sony has also launched a portable multimedia system as has Philips through its CDI 360, which is a standard CDI system based on a Motorola 68000 processor and running the OS/9 operating system. It has both NTSC and PAL outputs as well as its own active-matrix colour display measuring 6 inches across and is able to produce 756 by 556 pixel resolution images. As is the case with non-portable CDI players, it supports full motion video through hardware. This may sound effective but at $2,000, many will find it prohibitively expensive.

The initial problems with the development of a low-cost portable CD-ROM readers remain: conventional CD-ROM drives consume too much power, and compact LCDs (Liquid Crystal Displays) and the more costly colour TFT (Thin Film Transistor) displays are simply too expensive, thus limiting their size.

One solution to that last problem might lie in something which we will call a 'slide reader'. A small LCD display of around five to seven lines fixed on a vertical rail could be moved up or down at random to read the contents of whole pages. It is noticeable that attempts to produce such products thus far have relied on displaying complete pages – this is quite unnecessary when simply reading text.

With regard to the power consumption of CD-ROM drives, electronic memory (in the form of removable cartridges) can offer a suitable alternative. In fact, this is a possibility being exploited through several 'electronic book' projects at present. Text and graphics are made available in digital form early on in the modern publishing process, thus providing the necessary prelude to developing a CD-ROM. There is almost always a clause in book contracts requiring submission of word processed text files. Image files from scanners, video grabbers, graphics packages and so forth, are nowadays common.

For many publishers, however, CD-ROM is only viable through high-volume print runs beyond several thousand, or when the market can stand a high cover price, such as an encyclopedia, for instance. However, publishing a modest 250 page book retailing at the average market price is fast becoming viable as the installed CD-ROM user base grows.

2.2.3 Multimedia

There can be little doubt that the terms CD-ROM (or CD variant) and multimedia will become as inseparable as floppy disk and computer. By virtue of its immense storage capacity, CD-ROM currently provides a practical and affordable medium through which reasonably sophisticated multimedia can be distributed.

The large data storage capacity of CD-ROM so evident for textual applications diminishes considerably when placed in the perspective of multimedia. With diverse elements such as motion video and audio all mixed together, multimedia can be an awkward and space-consuming blend to digitise and store on DSM.

With a single (full-screen) frame of video consuming around 1,000 Kbytes, the problem of data storage capacity is appreciated (See Chapter 3). There is also a more fundamental problem in that the average data transfer rate between a traditional CD-ROM drive and computer is far too slow at 150 Kbytes/sec (See Section 2.4).

However, double-spin or dual-speed drives give an optional data transfer rate of 300 Kbytes/sec. Commercial examples include the NEC Intersect CDR74 and Apple CD300i. The yet higher performance six-disk multichanger Pioneer DRM-604X is specified as producing a continuous 600 Kbytes/sec. In independent tests[9], the DRM-604X transferred 60 Mbytes in a staggering 10 seconds, giving an average data transfer rate of 598 Kbytes/sec.

Although data transfer rates have increased dramatically, it remains a comparative bottle-neck, and represents a problem in regard to using CD-ROM for delivering video clips – and particularly FMFSV.

The solution to supporting motion video on CD-ROM lies in image compression, of which numerous techniques and technologies exist (See Chapter 3). The image compression algorithm used in Intel DVI, for example, operates by storing only those parts of a frame which are different from a previous one. Compression ratios achieved therefore depend upon the type of sequence being compressed.

Of course, it is not enough merely to compress video in isolation, as other elements of multimedia such as audio have to be considered. For instance, you cannot simply lay down audio according to the Red Book (or CD-DA) standard and encode compressed video elsewhere. If this were the case, audio could only be combined with interactivity, computer graphics and text (without temporarily storing audio first). In the light of this, data has to be interleaved, meaning that video and audio segments are combined on the same track (See Chapter 3).

With technical barriers surmounted, effective standards represent the next step toward accelerating the use of CD-ROM as a DSM for multimedia (See Chapter 3).

2.2.4 Databases

Databases have become synonymous with computer technology, where in recent years information on the printed page has been transcribed to magnetic storage media. A further migration to optical media now looks inevitable, and the creation of many new databases will almost certainly involve a decision concerning whether or not the end-product should reside on CD-ROM.

Many useful on-line databases are in the Gigabyte range. These can sometimes be stored on CD-ROM by daisy-chaining typically four to eight drives, from which it is then possible to access data randomly as from a single drive. The number of drives which can be daisy-chained varies according to manufacturer. An alternative to daisy-chaining is to use a magazine drive such as the Pioneer 6-Disc drive, which is capable of reading six disks simultaneously. Optical networks also provide a means of accessing multiple CD-ROM drives.

Database protection remains an issue for many publishers, and the notion of installing a CD-ROM system on-site increases the threat of illegal copying or unlicensed access. Encryption methods provide one solution to this, requiring the user's computer to be fitted with a decryption peripheral. These are very much like *dongles* – hardware devices which prevent unauthorised access to programs.

Product pricing is often a complex problem for database publishers, and traditional methods of charging users are usually perceived as unfair. Flat payment for a complete database installation, or yearly subscription fee, are two methods which are likely to leave either publisher or user dissatisfied.

A fairer costing system naturally takes into account the amount of service provided to the user. Return On Investment (ROI) owned by Personal Library Software Inc., is a hardware/software system which monitors each access to a database calculating a fee commensurate with usage.

A database comprising material owned by different organisations or contributors can also be handled using ROI technology. Owners of material will receive royalties calculated directly from customer usage. ROI therefore assists CD-ROM publishers in combining databases/information from different sources.

2.2.5 PhotoCD

A CD variant developed by Kodak in conjunction with Philips, and launched in 1992, PhotoCD permits the processing of 35mm photographic negatives into digital form. Kodak continues to licence high-street photographic finishers to develop conventional film reels into images on PhotoCD using a CD-R drive. Additional films can be processed and added to the same PhotoCD on up to 99 different occasions (99 being the maximum number of tracks supported). Following the addition of the second batch of images, it becomes a 'multisession' CD.

Photographs can be stored at a number of different resolutions, including 128 by 192, 256 by 384, 512 by 768, 1024 by 1536 and 2048 by 3072. Images of up to 18 Mb can be compressed down to 4.5 Mb without noticeable loss of quality.

Together with appropriate software, images on PhotoCD can be viewed using dedicated PhotoCD players, CD-ROM XA compatible drives, so-called XA-ready drives, CD-I players and multi-session CD-ROM drives. PhotoCDs can be read using conventional CD-ROM drives, but only one 'session' can be accessed and viewed. It should also be noted that XA-ready drives are not 100% CD-ROM XA compatible as many require additional interface circuitry to read interleaved data, which is the central theme of CD-ROM XA. Basically current XA-ready drives lack the ADPCM (Adaptive Delta Pulse Code Modulation) (See Chapter 3).

In addition to Kodak PhotoCD Access, Corel Draw, MS Word, Adobe PhotoShop, Shoebox and PhotoEdge are just some of many other software products able to open and read PhotoCD images. The future PhotoCD standard will be a multimedia one, where interleaved audio will be included, giving the ability to tag sound bites to images. Taking advantage of this development, it will be necessary to have a delivery system that incorporates ADPCM (See Chapter 3) circuitry.

2.3 CD-ROM drives

Though little appears to separate drives on the surface, deeper analysis reveals many subtle differences that govern overall performance. Data transfer rate, buffer size, access time, multi-session compatibility (see Section 2.2.5), XA compliance (see Section 2.2.5), and type of interface are just some of the features that separate drives.

Buffer size helps improve speed of operation by permitting the drive to search for and read data without waiting for the computer to accept all outgoing data. The buffer is simply an area of RAM (Random Access Memory) which acts as a temporary store between drive and computer. Buffer sizes of 64 Kbytes are common on inexpensive drives.

Average access time, a measure of how long it takes the laser head to locate and begin reading an appropriate region of disc, is measured in milliseconds (ms), and tends to vary from around 900ms down to about 200ms. Integral to access time, latency represents time taken for the read head to find the appropriate CD-ROM data block during random access. This tends to increase with turns of track farthest from the disc's centre. Typically, latency may vary from between 50 and 80ms for innermost turns, and approximate 150ms for outermost turns.

On inexpensive and, dare it be said, old fashioned drives, average data transfer rates vary little and can be assumed to be fixed at either 150 Kbytes/sec or 171 Kbytes/sec (See Section 2.4). More advanced dual-speed drives offer double this rate, and there is the state-of-the-art quadspeed drive, the Panasonic DRM-604X excel, which has a sustainable data transfer rate of around 600 Kbytes/sec. A less important area of difference concerns the maximum data transfer rate, which tends to be noticeably higher than the average. In fact, it can be more than four times greater. Maximum data transfer rate is achieved through burst transfer (or burst mode), where the drive seizes the computer processor time completely.

CD-ROM data is stored in the form of blocks that provide a means of storing information logically to yield a data structure which is both manageable and readable. Using one-hour discs, the two different user data block sizes of 2 Kbytes and 2.28 Kbytes in Mode 1 and Mode 2 operation, give 553 Mbytes and 602 Mbytes data capacities, respectively. All high specification drives support Mode 1 and Mode 2 operation, including that integrated into the CDTV.

Data capacities vary little, and using standard technology a maximum of around 660 Mbytes (See Section 2.4) can be achieved. Data capacity is not a function of drive architecture but of the disc itself; size of data blocks and play time dictate data storage capacity (See Section 2.4).

All modern drives PC drives can read discs encoded according to High Sierra Group (HSG) and ISO 9660 formats, both of which concern the storage of alphanumeric data. All but an extreme minority cope with these, and also double as audio CD players. Note, contrary to many articles which state categorically that High Sierra is the same as ISO 9660, there are subtle differences. For example, old fashioned High Sierra drives have existed which are unable to read some ISO 9660 discs. Other optical disc formats include Philips Compact Disc-Interactive (CDI) and the Apple Hierarchical Filing System (HFS). However, ISO currently remains most widespread, and can be seen in multimedia through Commodore's CDTV.

2.3.1 CD-ROM Drive Installation

Almost all desktop computers are designed with a view to future expansion, able to accommodate extra floppy disk drives, hard drives, fax cards, network cards and the many other popular peripherals. IBM PC XT, ATs and PS/2s, for example, include a number of expansion slots intended to accommodate such add-ons. The Macintosh is also expandable, with the II series a little more so than the Macintosh SE and Classic (See Chapter 3). However, external embellishments can always be accommodated due to the incorporation of a Small Computer Systems Interface (SCSI) on all Macintosh computers, which began with the Macintosh Plus.

CD-ROM drives can be either internal or external In Fig. 2.4, the new Texel internal and external drives (DM-3024 and DM-5024) are illustrated.

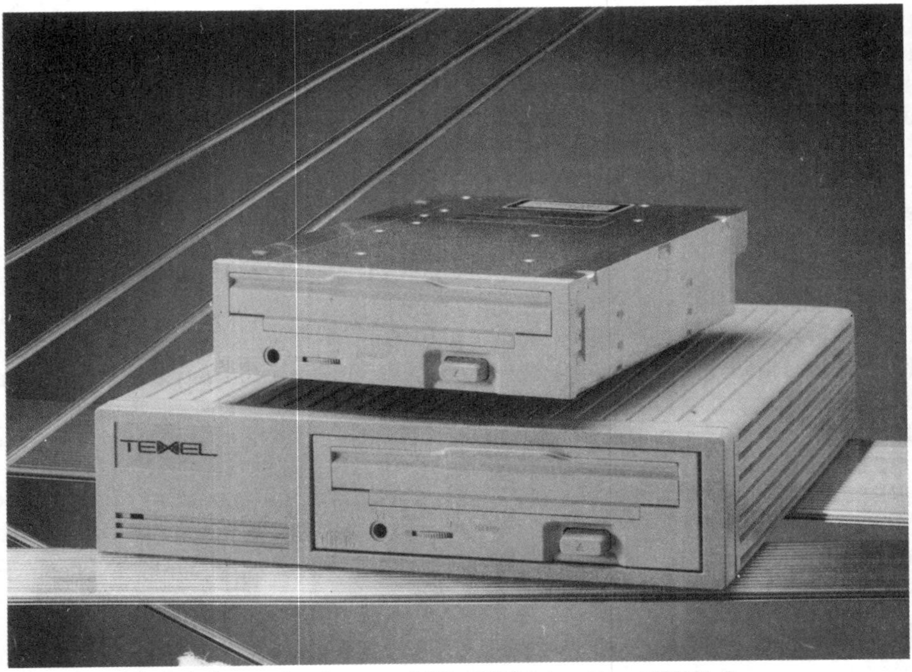

Fig 2.4: Internal and external CD-ROM drives from TEXEL Corp

Other than saving desk space and reducing the number of mains leads, there are no other advantages in using internal drives.

Lack of space or an insufficient power supply, can force the need for an external or portable drive (See Fig. 2.5). Indeed a number of desktop computers on the market support little more than two 3.5'' drive bays, as it seems that the advent of surface mount technology has encouraged some manufacturers to opt for yet smaller cases than ever before. Apple and Tandy led the small footprint computers, but IBM with its abnormally high profile are remembered as being the catalyst with its PS/2 range.

Fig 2.5: NEC external drive

Internal or external, the connection of a CD-ROM drive requires an appropriate interface, of which there are basically two kinds: proprietary bus interface and SCSI. The simplest interfaces are indigenous to particular drives, and include a proprietary bus connection. Using this technique, a PC XT/AT machine requires a different interface card from a PS/2 system or compatible. Similarly, neither of these interfaces would suit Apple computers, which require SCSI compatible drives. Proprietary bus interfaces are indigenous to different manufacturers, resulting in zero interchangeability between different drives. For example, you cannot simply swap between Hitachi and NEC drives.

Until 1991 all proprietary bus connections took place over an eight-bit bus, giving compatibility across the board in terms of PC XTs and ATs. For PS/2s and compatible systems, all of which possess the Micro Channel Architecture (MCA) bus, an appropriate MCA interface card is required.

SCSI is now universal and officially backed by ANSI (American National Standards Institute). Aimed to provide interchangeability between peripherals and computer systems from different manufacturers, it is not intended solely for the attachment of CD-ROM drives. It is often used to interface hard disk drives, printers and other peripherals. In fact, more and more devices now come with SCSI interfaces. SCSI implementations tend to vary in performance in terms of speed of input and output operations. For example, some controllers consist of the most basic bidirectional bus offering low data transfer speed, and in many instances they barely meet official SCSI requirements. SCSI controller cards can be fitted to PC XT/AT machines and PS/2s (and compatibles), where any SCSI drive (or compatible peripheral) can then be connected. Controller cards for PC XT/ATs and PS/2s permit the connection of seven peripherals and cost around £150 ($250). (Check your system or manual for the existence of such a card.)

The main advantage of a SCSI drive is interchangeability where, for example, it can be disconnected from an IBM PC or compatible machine and simply added to an Apple Macintosh. For this to be so, the authenticity and compatibility of the SCSI interface must be verified.

After physically adding a CD-ROM drive, it is necessary to indicate its presence by running an installation program. For IBM machines and compatibles, this will modify the DOS files AUTOEXEC.BAT and CONFIG.SYS files.

2.4 CD-ROM Operation

The underlying technology of CD-ROM is markedly similar to that used in Philips' first optical video disc system demonstrated in Eindhoven as early as 1972. This research and development led to LaserVision (See Section 2.8). CD-ROM is a reflective light system, where laser light is shone against turns of track which are encoded with digital data using pits and areas of land. Pits scatter the laser light, while areas of land produce reflected light. Reflected light is diverted to a photodetector that produces a series of electrical pulses corresponding to encoded data.

A CD-ROM disc rotates at a speed to provide a constant average read rate of at least 75 blocks/sec, though 150 block/sec or higher is preferable such that of dual-speed or quadspeed drive. Because data is embedded in the track (or tracks) of a CD-ROM at a uniform density (which equates to $0.6 * 10^6$ bits/mm^2), the disc must spin faster when the read head converges on its centre (and *vice versa*). This is quite unlike traditional vinyl audio discs which rotate at a constant angular velocity (CAV). The required constant linear velocity (CLV) is achieved by coordinating the position of the read head with speed of rotation using a simple feedback system.

The reason why standard drives operate in CLV mode rests firmly with the manner in which discs are encoded. It would have been equally possible to vary the distance between pits on a CD-ROM and so adopt a CAV system. There is a reasonable argument to suggest that CAV would have eliminated the need to vary motor speed and so reduce drive prices. However, experience of Philips LaserVision (videodisc) player indicates that almost twice as much data can be stored on a CLV disc.

Like all random-access, storage devices, encoded information has to be organised into manageable data blocks so as it may be located and retrieved. Irrespective of whether or not a disc uses one track or up to 99, CD-ROM data blocks of 2,352 bytes are used.

The amount of user data that CD-ROM data blocks provide is a function of Mode of operation. A Mode 1 disc, for example, will yield just 2 Kbytes (2,048 bytes) user data, while Mode 2 capacitates 2.28 Kbytes. Tables 2.1 and 2.2 show the CD-ROM data block structure in Modes 1 and 2 respectively. Mode 1's lower user data is due to demands imposed by error detection and correction codes. Conventional CD-DA (Compact disc – Digital Audio) data blocks comprise 2336 bytes of digital audio.

Table 2.1: Mode 1 block structure

Designation	Size	Byte number
Synchronisation	12 bytes	0 – 11
Header	4 bytes	12 – 15
User Data	2,048 bytes	16 – 2,063
Error detection	4 bytes	2,064 – 2,067
Space	8 bytes	2,068 – 2,075
Error correction code	276 bytes	2,076 – 2,351

Table 2.2: Mode 2 block structure

Designation	Size	Byte number
Synchronisation	12 bytes	0 – 11
Header	4 bytes	12 – 15
User Data	2,336 bytes	16 – 2351

The addition of error detection and correction codes makes Mode 1 discs more suited to data highly sensitive to error, such as computer software. In multimedia, Mode 2 is commonly used for the storage of video and audio data, as its accuracy is not so critical.

Storage capacity is increased in Mode 2 as is the average data transfer rate. The average user data transfer rate of a disc can be calculated by applying the following simple formula:

*Average user data transfer (Kbytes/sec) = blocks/sec * user block data (Kbytes)*

Mode 1:

Average user data transfer rate = 75 * 2

= 150 Kbytes/sec

Turning to Mode 2 discs, we have a noticeable improvement brought about through increased user block data:

Average user data transfer rate = 75 * 2.28

= 171 Kbytes/sec

Mode 2's percentage increase in user block data over Mode 1 is reflected in average data transfer rate. Hence the significance of user block data.

It should be pointed out that 'data transfer rate' and 'user data transfer rate' are quite different. Data sheets and drive specifications regularly opt for the former when they mean the latter. For example, in Mode 1, block data is significantly greater than user data largely because of the inclusion of error correction and detection code (ECC/EDC).

2.4.1 CD-ROM Addressing and User Data Capacity

CD-ROM addressing is carried out using measurements of time and data blocks read. Minutes, seconds and blocks provide enough information to locate any item of information. (Note, these are inherited directly from CD-DA). For example, considering a one hour CD-ROM, absolute addressing would take the following form:

minutes (M): 0 – 59
seconds (S): 0 – 59
blocks (B): 0 – 74

A track beginning mid-way through the CD-ROM, for instance, is addressed 29:29:37 (M:S:B). The length of a CD-ROM in minutes and the data block size in terms of user data, can be used to calculate user data capacity with pin-point accuracy. For example, consider the following simple formula:

*User data capacity = disc length (seconds) * blocks read/second * usable block data*

Applying this formula to calculate the precise data capacity of a one hour, Mode 1 disc gives:

User data capacity = 3600 * 75 * 2,048 bytes

= 552,960,000 bytes

= 527 Mbytes

Similarly, the capacity of a one-hour, Mode 2 disc:

User data capacity = 3600 * 75 * 2,336 bytes

= 630,720,000 bytes

= 602 Mbytes

User data capacity, besides being a function of user data block size, also depends upon disc play time. Though this can be up to about 79 minutes, the original Philips/Sony specification embodied a 60-minute play time.

Once again, it is important to recognise the difference between 'data capacity' and 'user data capacity', of which the former will always be significantly larger, and even more so using a Mode 1 disc. Drive specification sheets consistently fail to differentiate between the two.

2.5 CD-ROM Standards

Virtually all commercially successful technologies are products of workable standards able to unite manufacturers and yield a user base sharing a common bond. Two notable examples include video cassette players and audio CD players, both of which rapidly gained world-wide acceptance.

Often the path to standardisation is strewn with obstacles as manufacturers commit themselves to particular technologies or approaches. Sony, for instance, once backed the BetaMax VCR only to be squeezed out of the market by VHS players.

Left to industry, resultant standardisation need not be the best, but simply the one with most backing in terms of 'software'. It can be argued, for instance, that the immensely successful VHS video standard was quite inferior to competing technologies, and that the IBM PC was a far cry from being the best machine of its time.

For the developer, it is not necessary to understand the intricate detail of every (emerging) standard, but merely to be made aware of their existence, through which the necessary or largest market for a product can be addressed, which today means

ISO 9660. For example, an ISO 9660 title can often be converted between the PC, Macintosh or CDTV, by modifying the retrieval system alone (See Section 2.8).

The announcement of CD-ROM as a storage device in 1983 was accompanied by several fundamental problems, not least of which was a standard physical format and a standard file structure for storing alphanumeric data. There was also the problem of accessing the full data capacity of a CD-ROM through DOS, as existing versions were confined to storage devices with a maximum of 32 Mbytes. The world-wide standard and solution to this latter dilemma is thought of as the MS-DOS CD-ROM Extensions (See Section 2.6).

Created by Philips and Sony, The Yellow Book is an early standard dealing with the physical format of discs. Later, standard file structures came as a result of industry cooperation in 1985 by way of the High Sierra Group (HSG) standard. This was built upon by ISO to become ISO 9660. For applications devoid of video, and outside the boundaries of multimedia, ISO remains effective. Along with Apple HFS and CDI, it is accommodated by many replication companies. More recent standards to enter into mainstream CD usage include PhotoCD (1992) and CD-ROM XA (See Chapter 3).

2.6 MS-DOS CD-ROM Extensions

An additional device driver and an interface module developed to meet the demands of CD-ROM, are known as the MS-DOS CD-ROM Extensions (or MSCDEX). The CD-ROM Extensions enable exploitation of the full CD-ROM data capacity, as opposed to 32 Mbyte chunks.

Prior to the CD-ROM Extensions, the situation was all rather chaotic, with each drive manufacturer supplying programs that would swap individual 32 Mbyte data chunks. In one sense CD-ROM was actually being used like a number of small mass storage devices, negating its fundamental advantage. Commercial solutions to this problem did emerge, however. One of which came from TMS Inc., by way of LaserDos. This permitted access to the full data capacity, and also supported conventional DOS commands such as DIR.

2.6.1 Technical Overview

MS-DOS consists of a number of block device drivers able to support rewritable storage devices such as floppy disk drives and hard disks. These, however, are unsuitable for CD-ROM for several reasons:

- The full capacity of CD-ROM is not made available;
- MS-DOS utilities become inoperative because files and directories are not in the correct format;

- CD-ROM is not a rewritable medium;
- CD-ROM cannot take advantage of a standard File Allocation Table (FAT), because blocks are addressed differently (See Section 2.4.1);
- The assignment of drive letters to individual drivers is inappropriate.

MS-DOS, however, can accommodate a character device driver, which reads data as a stream of bytes, and is used to support serial devices such as modems. Unlike block device drivers, these are assigned names as opposed to drive letters. They do not support removable media, and do not accommodate multiple devices.

In essence, an effective CD-ROM device driver is a character device driver which has been modified to accommodate drive letters, an eight-byte character device name, and number of devices or units supported. The standard MS-DOS character device driver command set is enhanced to include commands specific to CD-ROM (See Table 2.3).

Table 2.3: Device driver command codes

Command Code	*Name*
0	INIT
3	IOCTL INPUT
7	INPUT FLUSH
12	IOCTLOUTPUT
13	DEVICE OPEN
14	DEVICECLOSE
128	READ LONG
129	Reserved
130	READ LONGPREFETCH
131	SEEK
132	PLAY
133	STOP PLAY

Commands 0, 3, 7, 12, 13, 14, 128, 130 and 131 are used to CD-ROM device drivers

Commands 132 and 133 are used to write device drivers that support audio

Commands 1, 2, 4, 5, 6, 8, 9, 10, 11, 15, 16 and 129 (not shown) are pertinent to block device drivers and will return an error code for unknown command

The installation of a CD-ROM driver requires an appropriate device entry in the CONFIG.SYS file which typically approximates the following:

DEVICE=\DEV\NEC.SYS/D:NEC001/N:1

Such a statement causes DOS to load the device driver NEC.SYS included in the DRIVE directory.

2.6.2 Device Driver Commands

For developers of device drivers, and readers that refuse to adhere to the 'black-box' concept, the following passages briefly run through the device driver commands.

To anyone writing a device driver, perhaps one of the first decisions which needs to be addressed is which Mode of operation to use. The READ LONG command (code 128) provides a *data read mode byte*, which is set to zero for Mode 1, and set to one for Mode 2. To reiterate, using modern high specification drives it can be assumed that both modes of operation are supported. READ LONG also accommodates an *addressing mode byte*, which can be assumed to be zero to invoke the HSG/ISO 9660 format.

READ LONG PREFETCH is intended to optimise access time by estimating which block is most likely to be read. In response to these estimates, the device driver positions the read head appropriately or caches relevant sectors.

IOCTL calls (commands 3 and 12) take care of the many mundane tasks that control a CD-ROM drive. They allow the application program to send control strings to the device driver. For example, IOCTL INPUT calls are used to retrieve information about the device. Similarly, IOCTL OUTPUT calls write CD-ROM specific commands to the device driver, such as eject disc, for example.

PLAY and STOP PLAY commands are relevant to audio tracks. The SEEK command simply positions the read head over appropriate disc locations. All MS-DOS device drivers require DEVICE OPEN and DEVICE CLOSE commands, without which they become incompatible and inoperable.

2.7 CD-ROM Networks

Local Area Networks (LANs) present a cost-effective multi-user environment in which computer resources and applications can be used to best effect. Based around a reasonably powerful file server, 'diskless workstations' (devoid of mass storage devices) or conventional computers provide multi-user access to many applications.

CD-ROM networks offer many of the same advantages of conventional LANs. A multi-user environment is created, and computer resources are put to optimum use. For example, databases on CD-ROM can be harnessed by up to a 100 LAN users on larger networks.

At the heart of the network lies an optical server which dynamically distributes requested information from CD-ROM drives to LAN users. For this reason, it has to be a relatively powerful high-end platform which today means a 386- or 486-based machine in terms of IBM compatible machines. The optical server is connected directly to CD-ROM drives, with some installations totalling 64 drives per server.

Where the maximum number of drives per server is exceeded, additional servers are employed. The incorporation of additional servers, prior to reaching the network maximum of drives per server, can lead to increased speed.

There are several commercially available CD-ROM network packages, many of which are software orientated. These are intended for installation on a LAN already in place, and run alongside the accompanying networking software. For example, Opti-Net from Online Computer Systems Inc., runs on the Novell network.

2.8 Retrieval Systems

CD-ROM data can only be made available through an appropriate retrieval system, of which many well-known implementations exist (See Appendix). A retrieval system takes the form of a program distributed on the disc itself and is most often installed to hard disk for the benefit of increased speed of operation. It can also be memory resident, loaded from disc each time the title is invoked. Proprietary systems, designed exclusively for a particular application or title, are also relatively common.

The combination of an exceptionally large amount of information, long access time and slow data transfer rate, renders retrieval system design of critical importance. Often providing a means of navigation, its suitability to the task in hand is just as important as the CD-ROM data itself.

As one would expect, retrieval systems are specific to applications, where the underlying design features vary considerably. At the simplest level, negotiating a telephone directory on CD-ROM merely requires the entry of simple search criteria. Wildcards or Boolean logic may also play a role. Such systems are termed target systems, and are useful for database applications.

Used in hypertext and hypermedia information structures, navigational systems are quite different. These enable the user to browse and navigate, repeatedly building upon searches in order to pursue specific paths.

2.8.1 Data Storage

Though the finality of a CD-ROM pressing means that developers are unlikely to get a second chance to re-organise data, it also means that encoded data will not be relocated following use.

Having looked at Mode 1 and Mode 2 discs and how average data transfer rates and data capacities are calculated, it is clear that drive specifications are really quite vague. They simply cannot be considered robust enough to withstand anything like the rigourous technical examination developers sometimes need to carry out regarding individual programs/applications.

Because CD-ROM drives are products of standardisation and therefore markedly similar, efforts to improve the performance of a program or application on invariably lie in optimising the data structure and retrieval software design. However, the developer cannot always be expected to understand the precise way in which such structures are developed, and it is therefore important that the relevant replication company is willing to pass on appropriate information and to give advice on software to be used in conjunction with data.

For example, data blocks residing in outer turns naturally fall victim to increased latency period, thus imposing a detrimental effect on access time. It is also important to note that, because discs are encoded at a uniform density, when filled to capacity, the greater proportion of disc data will occupy outer turns. Keeping related data in close proximity is also important, as this also reduces the average access time.

2.9 CD-R Technology

1992 saw the launch of more affordable CD-R drives, bringing low-volume CD-ROM publishing to the desktop. Undertaking this method of disc production makes the replication company redundant in the conventional sense. Though you may find that such companies offer various other useful production and consultancy services.

A number of writable CD technologies have emerged, including the familiar CD-WO (Write Once) disc whose specifications were issued by Philips and Sony in February 1988. There has also been erasable CD variants like the CD-THOR (Tandy High-intensity Optical Recording) dye-polymer disc.

The disc duplication process using CD-R is quite different from that adopted by commercial disc replication companies, as the creation of a master (see Chapter 5) is unnecessary. In effect, each and every writable disc produced using a CD-R drive is a master.

The prices of writable blank discs is falling, with the $40 price in 1992 falling to $25 by early 1993. Eastman Kodak (Rochester, NY) predicts $10 blanks in three years. PhotoCD is obviously the major force placing downward pressure on blank disc prices, as even a small penetration of the photo-processing market would greatly increase disc production requirements.

Sometimes, and provided they accept that your data is viable for resale in CD form, a replication company may produce your disc at their own expense and then sell them to you as and when you require at less than £20 each. Nimbus Information Systems (Weystone Leys, Gwent, UK) offer such agreements to selected publishers. There are also instances where the company will market and sell your CD product. Assuming a low RRP of say £50 per disc, it is common to produce around 1,000 copies.

Whether CD-R is a viable route obviously depends upon the volume of discs required. For example, if CD-R is to be adopted for archiving application where data is to be committed to a single CD-R disc (or perhaps duplicate copies) on a regular basis, then the services of a replication company are uncalled for. Alternatively, if you wish to duplicate less then 50 discs, CD-R may also be preferred.

2.9.1 CD-R operation

The substrate of a writable dye-polymer disc used with CD-R drives has a spiralling U-shaped groove called a pregroove, which is 600 nanometers wide and 100 nm deep. On top of this is an organic dye recording layer over which there is an gold reflective layer. Both layers are then coated with a top protective layer.

The writable disc is encoded by laser heating; CD-R drives use a laser beam of specific wavelength in order to heat the reflection, recording and substrate layers. The expanding substrate layer then impresses a fused recording layer so producing familiar pits and areas of land.

2.9.2 CD-R disc longevity

CD-ROMs and other pressed CD variants are well-known for their durability and long life. However, their aluminium layer, even though hermetically sealed by a protective lacquer, is prone to oxidisation in the long term. On the positive side, they are not vulnerable to relatively high temperatures.

With proper care and storage (in regard to heat) CD-R discs can be reasonably assumed to last up to 25 years. Although archival CD-R discs should probably by updated periodically at a frequency considerably less than 25 years. CD-THOR, a disc construction that is comparable to that of CD-R, is erased by heating.

One advantage of CD-R discs is that they normally have a gold reflection layer, which is a great deal more enduring than aluminium. There are also specialised tempered glass CD-R discs such as those manufactured by Digipress (Louisville, KY) which, though expensive, can last hundreds of years.

2.10 CD-ROM XA

Much has been written about CD-ROM XA, which has variously been described as 'a multimedia standard', 'a means of delivering multimedia elements concurrently' and so on. The rationale behind CD-ROM XA is simply to open up the computer and CD-ROM market to CDI. So-called XA-ready CD-ROM drives await the inclusion of an XA controller/adapter to be able to read CD-ROM XA discs. CD-ROM XA and CDI discs are not the same but are very similar in terms disc format and through the manner in which data is interleaved. Using ADPCM (Analogue Delta Pulse Code Modulation) audio and video data can be interleaved on the same track so providing a means of delivering them concurrently.

2.10.1 Audio and Sound

Red Book audio can be played through powered speakers, hi-fi system or television in the normal manner. But because a CD-ROM XA disc delivers audio, text, video, and computer graphics, the Red Book standard for CD-DA is often inappropriate. Audio and video data are interleaved on the same track, providing simultaneous delivery.

Essentially, there are two methods by which sound may be added to a CD-ROM XA multimedia title. The first of these is conventional, in that Red Book audio information is read directly from disc and played in real-time. The alternative computer-oriented technique involves writing audio data to RAM prior to playback. Called soundmaps, these provide a means of regurgitating frequently played audio sequences. And because RAM access times are typically less than 100 nano-seconds as opposed to hundreds of ms associated with CD drives, soundmaps can be invoked almost instantly. The CDI Full Functional Specification or Green Book, of which CD-ROM XA is a subset, sets out three audio quality levels:

A-Level audio: equivalent to the first play of a vinyl disc under optimum conditions, minus noise caused by static and physical stylus contact. A more compact representation of audio CD data, it requires approximately half the information of CD-DA. An entire disc would give a maximum of two hours A-Level stereo playback.

B-Level audio: equivalent to a high quality stereo FM broadcast transmitted under optimum conditions. An entire CDI disc gives a maximum of four hours B-Level stereo playback.

Note: depending upon speakers, amplification and the listener, users are sometimes unable to differentiate between A-Level audio and B-Level audio.

C-Level audio: equates to an AM radio broadcast transmitted under optimum conditions. A whole disc could yield over 16 hours playing time.

2.10.2 CD-ROM XA Sectors, Data Transfer Rate and Data Capacity

The first and most obvious identifying factor of a CD-ROM XA disc is its format, which deviates slightly from CD-ROM. A typical CD-ROM consists of Mode 1 (cooked mode) and Mode 2 (raw mode) data blocks. XA discs include Form 1 and Form 2 sectors that exist in Mode 2. CD-ROM XA sectors, each comprising 2,352 bytes raw data, can be read at a standard (CLV) read rate of 75 sectors/sec.

Like Mode 1 blocks, Form 1 sectors contain error detection and error correction codes. They are useful, therefore, where data integrity is essential, i.e. program data. A Form 1 sector yields 2,048 bytes user data. The absence of such codes from Form 2 sectors makes them useful for data which is less susceptible to error, i.e. audio and video data. Form 2 sectors yield 2,324 bytes of user data as opposed to the standard 2,336 bytes associated with Mode 2 data blocks.

Form 2 sectors deliver less user data because of the inclusion of a sub-header which contains identifying code. These codes indicate the data type of each sector, and they help increase the speed of reading interleaved data. Because of the additional sub-header, Form 2 sectors yield lower data capacities and data transfer rates than CD-ROM Mode 1 blocks.

The average data transfer rate yielded by CD-ROM XA Form 1 and Form 2 sectors can be calculated using the formula established in Chapter 2:

*Average user data transfer rate = sectors/sec * usable sector data (bytes)*

Form 1 equals Mode 1 operation, thus:

Average user data transfer rate = 75 * 2,048

= 153,600 bytes/sec

= 150 Kbytes/sec

Form 2:

Average user data transfer rate = 75 * 2,324

= 174,300 bytes/sec

= 170.2 Kbytes/sec

Calculating exactly how much can be stored on a CD-ROM XA disc, or any disc for that matter, is complex when considering interleaved data. Note, authoring systems/tools can keep the CD-ROM XA designer abreast with available data capacity during development.

We can calculate raw data capacity (of a one-hour disc, for example) by applying the following simple formula:

Data capacity (Kbytes) = *disc length (seconds) * sectors/blocks per second * sector/block data*

= 3,600 * 75 * 2,352 bytes

= 635,040,000 bytes

= 605 Mbytes

Turning to user data:

User data capacity = *disc length (seconds) * sectors/blocks per second * user sector/block data*

User data capacity (Form 1) = 3,600 * 75 * 2,048 bytes

= 552,960,000 bytes

= 527.3 Mbytes

One hour, Form 2 disc:

User data capacity (Form 2) = 3,600 * 75 * 2,324 bytes

= 627,480,000 bytes

= 598.4 Mbytes

In reality, the CD-ROM XA disc format is said to support about 650 Mbytes storage capacity. For example, a Form 2 disc with a playing time of 65 minutes, 12 seconds:

User data capacity (Form 2) = 3,912 * 75 * 2,324 bytes

= 681,861,000 bytes

= 650.2 Mbytes

Many regard XA as a bridge between CDI and the PC. However, it would be equally possible to develop decoders for other machines, such as the Macintosh and Amiga. In fact, these machines offer a great deal more technical excellence in terms of graphics and sound than most standard PCs.

Whether we will see such developments, and just how compatible they will be with the CDI Full Functional Specification, is unanswerable at this time. However, such options and possible advancements *are* possible and should be borne in mind.

Though CD-ROM XA is not 100% compatible with CDI, it is possible to develop dual-format discs which can be played on both CDI and CD-ROM XA systems. CD-ROM XA decoders for the PC are unable to deliver A-Level audio, but offer the advantage of 80-column text and better picture definition for certain other detailed visuals.

2.11 Origins of CD-ROM

All too often a potted history of CD-ROM begins with its announcement in October 1983. Leading up to this climax, however, a great deal of research and development took place. Its line of development is traceable because one company, namely Philips, can be accredited with many of the widely recognised milestones.

Initially there was no long term plan to speak of, but just a drive to find an efficient means of storing still or moving images on disc. Associated projects instantly became known as videodisc experiments. The term had nothing whatever to do with optical storage techniques but simply referred to the fact that images were being stored on disc.

In the early sixties, Decca and Telefunken had some success with short recordings using vinyl discs and spiral grooves. As anticipated, the high speed of rotation required, led to rapid wear of both disc and stylus. The American RCA and Zenith corporation solved the problem of wear with the Capacitance Electronic Disc (CED) system. Here, the disc surface and stylus were used to represent the plates of a capacitor whose charge varied as the stylus passed over grooves on the disc.

With the transition of the laser (light amplification by stimulated emission of radiation) from being an awkward and bulky gas-filled tube to a low-powered and more compact light emitting diode in the fall of 1962, experiments with optically encoded discs began. First, transparent discs were tried, including a floppy disc system which was to prove ineffective. Then in 1972 at Eindhoven, Philips demonstrated a reflective light system which was to mark the birth of practical optical discs. This led to the commercial launch of LaserVision (videodisc player) in 1978 (US) and in 1982 (Europe).

LaserVision was originally intended as a consumer product for playing films/videos. Coupled with the paucity of films available on LaserVision disc, the fact that programmes could not be recorded seemed to outweigh the advantages of durable discs and improved picture and sound quality. However, LaserVision survives today as a consumer product (more so in the US than in Europe) and also exists in IV/multimedia applications.

Supporting random access the videodisc player showed how still and motion video could be integrated into a computer environment, thus providing interactive video.

Thorn-EMI VHD players using a CED-type system developed by JVC, were less successful than LaserVision.

In terms of technology, LaserVision can be considered as a rather large CD-ROM drive where data is stored in analogue form. The more mature 12'' disc format comprises a spiral track about twelve miles long (which yields 54,000 adjacent turns) and is capable of storing two hours of video in CLV mode.

Launched in 1982, CD-DA capable of storing high-quality digital audio, virtually eliminated vinyl disc production by 1990. Its immense success can be attributed to the Philips/Sony Red Book Standard thus promoting the necessary compatibility. Subsequent mass production of CDs imposed considerable influence upon the development of CD-ROM. CD-ROM was announced as an 'information storage medium' by Philips and Sony in October 1983, with the standard physical format issued in June 1985.

Lack of a standard file format for storing alphanumeric data was one of the earliest and most expected obstacles to discourage publishing on CD-ROM. With a meeting of industry representatives in 1985 at the High Sierra Hotel at Lake Tahoe, Nevada, a standard was agreed. Now part of CD-ROM folklore the meeting resulted in the High Sierra Group (HSG) standard format for alphanumeric files.

By 1987 HSG was built upon by ISO, officially calling it ISO 9660. This acted not only as a catalyst for the development of CD-ROM based applications but also stimulated drive manufacture. Philips, Sony, Hitachi and NEC are some of many manufacturers that produce ISO drives.

2.11.1 A Prelude to the Origins of CD-ROM

"I have heard articulate speech produced by sunlight! I have heard a ray of the sun laugh and cough and sing!...Can imagination picture what the future of this invention is to be!" – Alexander Graham Bell, February 26, 1880

The history of CD-ROM is by no means a contemporary one, or to be more precise it is not as contemporary as pioneering companies involved with its development are so keen to state. If we were to go right back to the beginning, we would have to discuss the development of light as a means of communication and its steady diffusion into the electronics industry. In fact, we would have to go back to the nineteenth century.

In 1880 the prophecy that light would one day be used for transmission purposes over hundreds of miles was met with cynicism. Like then, if ten years ago someone told you that the vinyl disc would soon be replaced by an optically encoded medium occupying little more than the palm of your hand, you might have expressed doubts. If at the same time you were told that by the end of the decade desktop computers would include optical storage devices supporting some 660 Mbyte data storage capacity, you would have expressed further doubts.

The fact is light has long since been appreciated as a means of communication. In the afternoon of February 19, 1880, Alexander Graham Bell and Sumner Tainter, his laboratory assistant, managed to transmit a voice over a beam of light. The transmission over 213 metres was achieved from the roof of the Franklin School House in Washington, D.C. to Bell's laboratory at 1325 L Street. After the experiment, Bell concluded that it was his most important invention. Whether he simply said this in the excitement of the moment, or whether he really did foresee its potential is difficult to gauge.

This demonstration of lightwave communication was (and is) plagued by interference problems caused by the earth's atmosphere. It is not clear if Bell failed to see these problems, or whether he thought they would be surmounted, but the solution of using some kind of fibre optic cable seemed to evade his recorded thoughts. Ironically, this concept was presented unwittingly by a cynical journalist, with incredible foresight as it so happens. After describing Bell as a man who invented a good deal of the telephone, the journalist wrote, ". . . Does Professor Bell intend to connect Boston and Cambridge ... with a line of sunbeams hung on telegraph posts, and, if so, what diameter are the sunbeams to be, and how is he to obtain the required size?"

If it were not so sarcastic, it seems just the sort of anonymous and controversial letter Bell himself might have written to gain patronage for his invention. Of course fibre optic cable is buried beneath the ground today as opposed to hung from poles.

The current explosion in lightwave communication can be attributed to several contemporary inventions, which though concentrated in the sixties, finally came to a head in 1979 with the refinement of fibre optic cable by Japan's Nippon Telegraph and Telephone Public Corporation, who developed a silica fibre which performed with a loss of just 0.2 dB per kilometre.

The laser was perhaps the most significant advancement when we consider the prelude to CD-ROM technology. It is the coherence of laser light (aided by lenses and mirrors) which provides the degree of focus required to read minute portions of CD variants. The steady convergence of optical devices and electronics resulted in optronics, which laid the foundation for the emergence of the familiar continuum, including LaserVision, CD-DA, CD-ROM, CD-V, CDI, CD-ROM XA and PhotoCD.

The evolution of multimedia technology has travelled a complete circle. The availability of Interactive TeleVision (ITV) is due to fibre optics. The enormous bandwidth of optical cables enables multimedia and ITV to be brought into homes.

3

Multimedia Delivery

This chapter deals with the hardware that goes to make up an MPC, showing how to develop, or to buy, a multimedia system that best suits your needs or your pocket. It also deals with multimedia environments, as well as alternatives to the MPC such as PC-based CD-ROM XA systems. If you simply want to get to grips with the mechanics of PC multimedia, then you might like to skip section 3.1 which deals with graphics, video and related standards. This section might be seen as a little too involved if you have bought this book as a practical guide to PC multimedia.

The MPC has become a popular platform for multimedia with numerous high quality titles marketed and sold by leading companies such as Microsoft and The Software Toolworks. The quality of MPC titles is improving gradually, with noticeable strides forward being made in the educational variety. The popular Microsoft Musical Instruments, for example, has won widespread acclaim for its technical excellence. An encyclopedia of musical instruments from around the world, together with numerous recordings that are played through the sound card.

PC manufacturers have moved quickly in favour of multimedia peripherals and features. In 1992, for instance, Wang incorporate a sound recording and playback facility into the mainboard of one of its PC 461/33C. Supplied with a microphone this facilitate voice annotation in the Windows environment. But it is not just the PC that has taken multimedia into the marketplace. Numerous manufacturers have risen to the challenge of modern multimedia through several major initiatives including Philips CDI, CD-ROM XA, Intel DVI (Digital Video Interactive) or Intel i750 chipset, Commodore CDTV, and the Multimedia PC (MPC). Appliances such as CDI, CDTV and Tandy VIS (Video Information System) are aimed at the consumer market.

Numerous multimedia peripherals and packages have also appeared for the Apple Macintosh Computers. The software product QuickTime has become a standard method of producing motion video (MV) on the Macintosh platform, a version of which now exists for Microsoft Windows. The MPC equivalent to QuickTime is Microsoft's VfW, and numerous Windows video recorders use this as a basis for video capture and playback. Multimedia environments have also appeared, namely multimedia extensions for both Microsoft Windows 3.1 (or later) and IBM OS/2 2.1 (or later). These provide control over various devices including sound cards, videodisc and CD-ROM drives.

Wang PC461/33C with sound recording and playback facility built into the mainboard.

Irrespective of whether multimedia systems physically resemble a desktop computer, they remain microcomputer based. Commodore CDTV, for example, is designed around the successful Amiga computer.

Multimedia systems fall into two main categories: 'plug-in-and-play' systems such as CDTV and CDI players, and those based upon conventional desktop computers such as the PC, Macintosh or Commodore Amiga. The latter fall into further groupings based upon how video is stored. For example, video can be stored either using an analogue videodisc player, or in digital form using a random access DSM such as magnetic hard disk, CD-ROM or other CD variant.

Considerably less expensive plug-in-and-play systems restrict usage to multimedia delivery, reading CD-ROM or CDI titles, playing audio CDs and, if multisession compliant, viewing PhotoCDs. All high specification CD-ROM drives and CDI players offer downward compatibility with CD-DA (Red Book standard) and are thus able to play audio Cds.

Plug-in-and-play systems can be further divided into portable systems, and non-portable or desktop systems. Portable multimedia players include the Philips CDI 360 and the Sony MMCD both of which emerged in 1992. These are very different appliances; the Philips system has a sophisticated 6 inches across active-matrix colour display capable of 756 * 556 pixel resolution while the MMCD has a 300 by 200 pixel display. However, Sony's solution currently retails at half the price of the CDI 360 in the US.

3.1 Graphics

The advancement of computer graphics has unleashed numerous computer applications ranging from Computer Aided Design (CAD) to colour desktop publishing (DTP). Through the coupling of high-resolution colour monitors and high specification graphic controllers, truly photographic quality images are now possible.

Built up of digitally defined pixel elements, computer images are invariably complex. For example, a 1024-by-768 pixel image yields 786,432 individual pixels. In a worst possible scenario situation, digitising such a black and white image would require a corresponding number of bits, or 98,304 bytes (786,432/8), or 96 Kbytes (98,304/1024). Progressing to a grey-scale arrangement using bits per pixel to give 256 (2^8) grey shades, the same 1024 by 768 pixel image requires 768 Kbytes – eight times the storage capacity of its black-and-white equivalent.

256-colour graphics are an excellent exchange for eight-bit grey-scale. Crude four-bit, 16-colour images which consume as much as a quarter of the capacity, prove wholly inadequate to emulate the subtle colour graduations of a photograph.

Such is the complexity of photographic quality images, a minimum of 24-bit colour graphics are required. Red, green and blue are each represented by eight bits, thus facilitating the selection of 256 tones of each. By combining each colour component, over 16.7 million (256 * 256 * 256) colours are made available.

Yet higher quality results are achieved using 32-bit graphics where a further eight bits are used to control the degree of transparency of each pixel. Apple call this the Alpha Channel. Such state-of-the-art graphics on a 1024 by 768 pixel resolution monitor means that a single frame may consume as much as 3,072 Kbytes. Large image files of this sort are costly to process, transmit and store. They are also slow to transfer from computer to screen, as well as to and from hard disk. A solution to these problems lies in image compression.

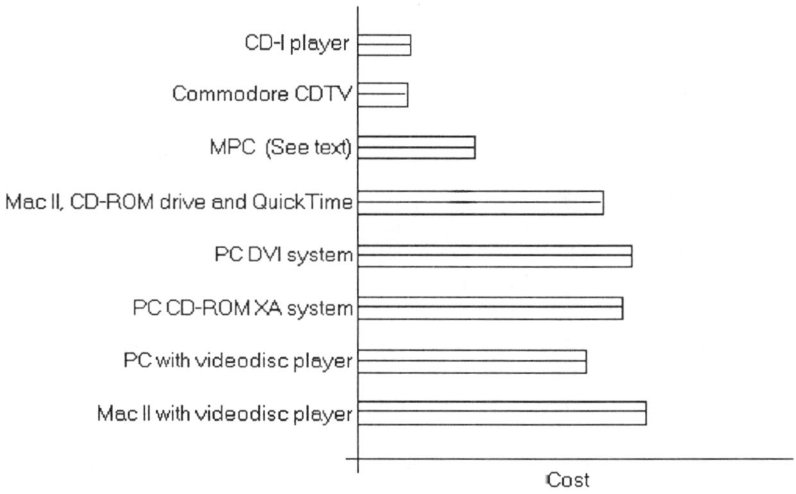

Fig 3.1: price guidelines (likely to change – check first)

3.1.1 Image Compression

Numerous image-compression techniques have been tried and tested over the years, where compression ratios of around 50 per cent often proved adequate. The sheer volume of data needed for 24-bit images and motion video manifests a need for compression ratios many orders of magnitude greater. Of numerous image-compression processes, the Discrete Cosine Transform (DCT) method has proved most popular. This method is adopted by numerous manufacturers and is the mainstay of the JPEG algorithm (discussed later in this section). A 'lossy' technique in that redundant pixel data is omitted, the DCT process involves transformation of image data from the spatial domain into the frequency domain.

In the spatial domain, pixels are defined in terms of X and Y coordinates, pixel intensity and/or colour. It is from here that the DCT process normally extracts appropriately 'sized' pixel arrays. Then, through two matrix multiplications a spatial-to-frequency transformation is achieved, where the resultant image data is represented according to the varying light-frequencies of the image.

Such matrix multiplication invariably requires intensive processing, and it is here that the limitations of conventional desktop machines have emerged yet again. Only on parallel processing systems, such as the transputer-based Meiko Computing Surface, can reasonably efficient image-compression programs be supported without the addition of pixel processors or processors with a math bias. Intel originally used the Computing Surface at its Princeton Operation for compressing motion video for DVI development.

On current PCs an additional processor (incorporated in a video capture board) is needed to meet the processing demands of the level of image compression required for FMFSV. The complexity of image compression is appreciated when considering that a single 8-by-8 matrix transformation which takes 512 multiplications. If it takes 4 matrix transformations to 'DCT' an 8-by-8 pixel array, then 2048 individual multiplications are required. Using specifically designed processors, matrix multiplications can be optimised by incorporating an appropriate instruction set, and by implanting coefficients to make up transformation matrices on the chip itself. A number of such image processors have emerged including the Inmos A121, Intel i750 chip set (DVI), Intel i860 and i870 and the C-Cube Microsystems CL550.

The various hardware and software solutions for still-image compression led to a need for a sufficiently advanced and standard algorithm. Sponsored by the ISO, it fell upon the Joint Photographics Experts Group (JPEG) to do just that.

The JPEG algorithm is symmetrical (See Fig 3.2) in that the number of processes constituting image compression mirrors those of decompression. Equally complex, image compression and decompression times are optimised through hardware implementations.

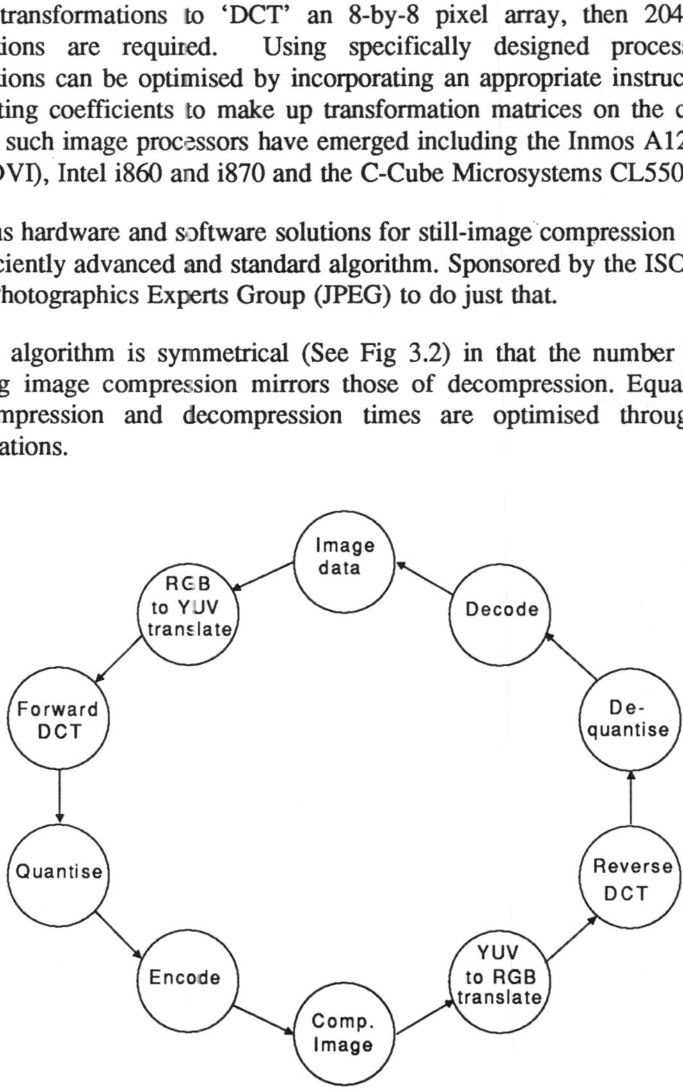

Fig 3.2

The JPEG algorithm is a combination of 'lossy' and lossless image-compression techniques. Lossless compression processes such as Huffman and Run Length Coding (RLC) take place in the spatial domain. However, because the DCT process is responsible for the greater part of the compression ratio, the algorithm is collectively referred to as being 'lossy'.

The C-Cube Microsystems CL550 image processor chip is frequently used to implement the JPEG algorithm and it is incorporated in add-ons made by various manufacturers. Up until the end of 1990, C-Cube Microsystems manufactured the CL550-based Compression Master board for both the Macintosh and PC. This is capable of a 75:1 image compression ratio.

The need for compression devices is growing as more and more workstation manufacturers (such as NeXT) incorporate hardware implementations of the JPEG algorithm. Though the JPEG algorithm was initially aimed at still-image compression, it is often applied to motion video. Indeed a growing number of JPEG adapters are appearing for the Macintosh and the PC. Numerous graphics programs for the PC now support the JPEG format.

3.1.2 Digital Motion Video

Motion video is the most animating feature of modern multimedia. Using videodisc players it has been possible to incorporate FMFSV in a computer environment for some time. However, here we look at digital video and how it can be stored on CD-ROM.

Because multimedia is a blend of concurrent processes, its storage on a single optical disc requires various elements to be interleaved on the same track. Before this concept could be addressed, the inability of conventional (serial) desktop computers to play motion video stored on CD-ROM, represented a significant hurdle. Reasons as to why this is not possible lie in the inadequate rate at which data is transferred from CD-ROM to computer (See Chapter 2), and in inadequate data storage capacity.

Consider some practical figures and current technology. A single frame of full-screen video when digitised may take up about 750 Kbytes. Therefore, around 30 seconds of video, running at 30 fps, can be reaped from a single standard CD-ROM.

The real problem, however, is the inadequate data transfer rate between a standard CD-ROM drive and computer, and not inadequate data storage capacity. The average Mode 1 data transfer rate of 150 Kbytes/sec (See Chapter 2) yielded by the much of the installed CD-ROM drive base is desperately slow, yielding just one frame every few seconds.

A blanket solution to both problems lies in image-compression. For example, if frames of video are compressed significantly, then the need for large data storage capacity and, more importantly, high rates of data transfer is reduced.

Intel has refined such a technology, acquired from General Electric in October 1988. Called Digital Video Interactive (DVI), its home is the Intel Princeton Operation, which is part of the Microcomputer Components Group. Digital Video Interactive (DVI) originally began in the David Sarnoff Research Centre, New Jersey – the once RCA laboratories. Aimed at the PC AT and PS/2, DVI works on a simple premise: only those parts of a frame which are different from a previous frame are stored. As a result, up to 72 minutes of full-screen, full-motion video (at 30 fps) can be stored on a single 12 cm CD-ROM disc. Alternatively, DVI can be used to store 44 hours of near-AM (Amplitude Modulation) audio, or, 650,000 pages of A4 text, or, 40,000 medium resolution video stills.

The problems associated with motion video are not 'machine specific' but universal. Machines with superior graphics capability such as high end Macintosh computers face an identical bottle-neck in terms of insufficient data transfer rates and inadequate processing power.

3.1.3 Motion Video Standards

The early days of multimedia were plagued by the problem of just how digital video data should be compressed. A need arose for international standards for the digital storage and retrieval of interleaved video and audio data.

Sponsored by the ISO and CCITT (Committée Consultitif International Telegraphique et Telephonique), the Motion Picture Experts Group (MPEG) was given the task of developing a standard coding technique for moving pictures and associated audio. The group was separated into six specialist sub-groups including Video Group, Audio Group, Systems Group, VLSI Group, Subjective Tests Group and DSM Group.

The first phase of MPEG work covered DSMs with up to 1.5 Mbits/sec transfer rates, for storage and retrieval, advanced Videotex and Teletext, and telecommunications. The second phase of work addressed DSMs with up to 10 Mbits/sec transfer rates for digital television broadcasting and telecommunications networks. This phase would cling to the existing CCIR 601 video resolution, with audio transfer rates up to 128 Kbits/sec.

MPEG participants include leaders in: computer manufacture (Apple Computer, DEC, IBM, Sun and Commodore); consumer electronics; audio-visual equipment manufacture; professional equipment manufacture; telecom equipment manufacture; broadcasting; telecommunications; and VLSI manufacture. University and research establishments also play an important role.

3.2 Multimedia systems and appliances

Many subtle (and sometimes major) differences separate the various multimedia systems which are commercially available. The most notable difference is between the plug-in-and-play systems and those based upon conventional desktop computers such as the MPC.

Though more expensive, desktop computer-based systems generally offer superior display and can also be upgraded to authoring stations (See Chapter 4). The transformation from MPC to MPC authoring station may require the inclusion of a sufficiently large hard disk, a suitable video capture board, and an appropriate authoring tool or system.

User-interaction takes place via a mouse, remote control device or touch-screen. Touch-screens are less common but can be found on some systems including the Sony VIW-5600, which conforms to being a multimedia system and is used extensively as a geographic information system.

Because of the superior graphics capabilities and support from third-party manufacturers, Macintosh computers are particularly suitable for multimedia and also for applications within the area as a whole. HyperCard can be used to develop complete hypermedia applications as well as retrieval systems or user-interfaces for CD-ROM data.

Being a refined and particularly innovative design, the Macintosh naturally wields a higher market price. Apple Computer, however, moved toward breaking down its high end strategy in 1990, releasing a range of affordable Macintosh computers. In 1984, a Macintosh with 128 Kbytes RAM cost nearly $2,500. By 1991, the Macintosh Classic with 2 Mbytes RAM and 40 Mbyte hard disk was less than $1500.

Plug-in-and-play systems such as Commodore CDTV, Tandy VIS and CDI players are extremely low-cost, and are often used in conjunction with conventional televisions. At the time of its launch in 1991 CDTV was priced at around £599 ($999 US). One of the critical questions that needs to be asked when investing in an multimedia system or appliance is, ‘How long will it be before it becomes obsolete?’ For example, will the system purchased be served with interesting software for a reasonable period.

Software support for a product, a manufacturer’s ability to set industry standards, and the observance of agreed international standards, play important roles. For instance, lack of software proved a fatal for the BetaMax VCR. These events may well be echoed in the early stages of multimedia. However, the degree to which they occur rather depends on how effectively standards are implemented.

Fortunately, the MPC is served by a vast array of titles, and though like all PCs its subsystems can become outmoded, it can almost always be upgraded. For example, you may wish to include a larger hard disk, or move up from an 8-bit sound card to a 16-bit variant that delivers CD quality sound. Most important of all, the MPC is standard system and has the backing of Microsoft, the most influential PC software producer today.

3.3 PCs

PCs come in many different shapes and forms, ranging from so-called palmtops that are little bigger than a pencil box to large desktop computer systems. Desktop systems may feature a full-tower, mid-tower, mini-tower, slimline desktop or conventional desktop case.

Fig 3.3: PC with mini-tower case

Portable A4-size or notebook PCs have become widespread today, and now feature some of the most advanced hardware features that you would expect to find in desktop systems – but you pay a great deal more for them. Normally powered by rechargeable batteries, which last up to four hours on more expensive variants, they often feature power management which shuts down the screen and sometimes processor, too, during periods of inactivity.

Today, the cheapest and most basic portables use 386SX processors and a back-lit LCD (Liquid Crystal Display) with VGA (Video Graphics Array) compatibility. These displays usually produce either 16, 32 or 64 levels of grey. Generally such notebooks will weigh around three to four Kilograms.

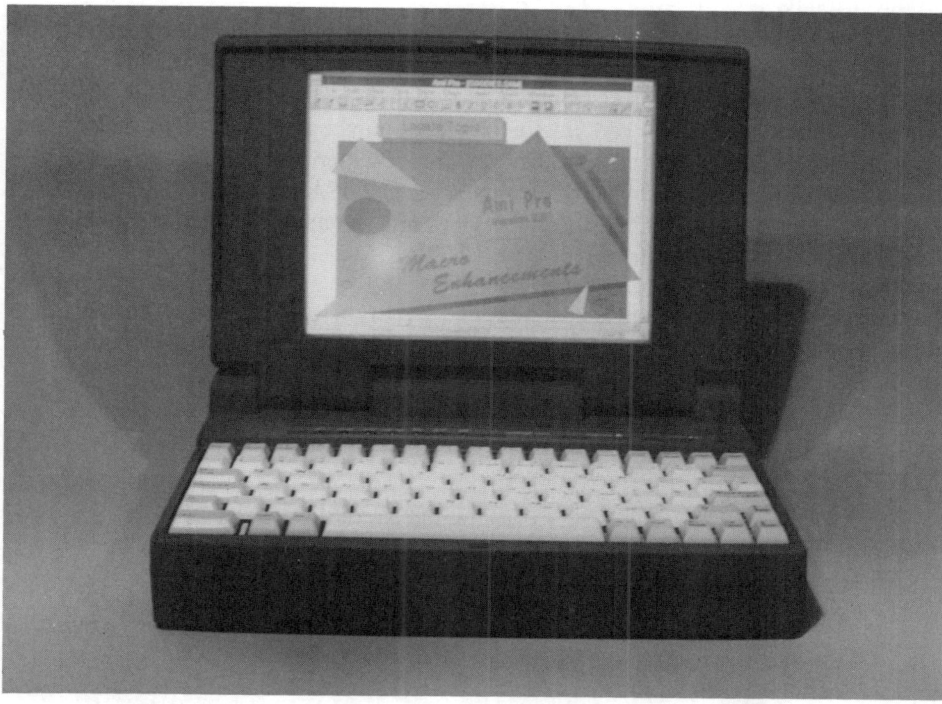

Fig 3.4: Low-cost notebook PC

More advanced notebooks feature 486 processors, local bus graphics, TFT (Thin Film Transistor) colour displays capable of producing 1024 * 768 pixels resolution, removable hard disks, built in trackball, and even have the ability to drive an external monitor at 1024 * 768 pixels resolution.

Modern notebooks have 65-pin PCMCIA (Personal Computer Memory Card International Association) slots which connect with almost credit card size peripheral devices. The exact dimensions of a PCMCIA card are, 8.5cm * 5.5cm, and their thickness may be either 3.3 mm, 5 mm or 10.5 mm. Memory cards are 3.3 mm thick, I/O devices are 5 mm thick and hard disks are 10.5 mm thick.

The original PCMCIA was designed for memory cartridges only, but in September 1991 PCMCIA Type II (PCMCIA 2.0) were launched facilitating hard disks and modem/facsimile devices.

However, though the PCMCIA laid down a hardware specification for slots and cards it did not specify a software interface, so many PCMCIA cards are proprietary. To solve this Intel introduced a standard interchangeable card aimed at Intel based machines. Called Exchangeable Card Architecture (ExCA), third-party manufacturers are free to use the logo provided their cards ExCA compliant.

As if to highlight the importance of miniaturisation and portability, sub-notebooks are becoming increasingly popular and often weigh less than half that of an A4 notebook. Most notebooks of whatever size feature optional docking terminals. This allow the whole computer to be plugged into a bay that may be connected to an external monitor and keyboard as well as other standard PC peripherals. The bay may also have an expansion chassis which contains a normal ISA (or alternative) expansion bus. So many standard MPC peripheral devices may be added including sound cards, video cards and CD-ROM drives.

An unusual docking terminal is that supplied by Ergo with its unique portable (but not battery powered) Ergo Brick. This solidly built system is built to withstand the rigours of working in harsh environments.

Fig 3.5: Ergo Brick PC with docking terminal

In 1991, at the sixth annual Multimedia and CD-ROM conference, Microsoft and Tandy unveiled the Multimedia PC (MPC) brand and logo. (Microsoft originally announced the MPC standard in mid 1990.) CompuAdd, AT&T, Olivetti Systems and Networks, NEC and Zenith agreed to produce MPCs.

World-wide presence and competitiveness of the PC industry as a whole, are just two advantages of PC multimedia. The fact that an MPC can be achieved by building upon numerous installed PCs is also significant.

Because of the many different PC configurations possible and the emergence of numerous IBM standards, a machine described as IBM-compatible tells little about its true identity. The objective of this section, therefore, is to reveal the many different system configurations available, and so provide adequate information for systems development. The Multimedia PC specification embodies the following minimum system/software requirements:

- 386SX processor or higher
- 2 Mb Ram
- 30 Mb hard disk
- CD-ROM drive with CD-DA (CD-Digital Audio) output and sustained 150 Kb/sec data transfer rate with 1 second access time while not using more than 40% of the CPU's processing power and MPC-compatible sound board
- MS-DOS 3.1 or higher
- Windows 3.1 or Windows 3.0 with Microsoft multimedia extensions
- MS-DOS CD-ROM Extensions (MSCDEX) version 2.2 or higher – if you do not have this and you are using MS-DOS 6.0 check your DOS directory
- Sound card – without this you can access text and graphics only
- Headphones or speakers

While this will deliver MPC titles, you will find that better results are achieved using systems that have 4 Mb of Ram and 'double-spin' CD-ROM drives (See Chapter 2). A 486SX processor (or higher) is also desirable.

3.3.1 PC Processors and mainboards

Nowadays with the vast array of processors available it is not enough to state that a machine is either 386 or 486-based. The many different processor variants available leads to a whole host of MPC specifications. Add to this the wide variety of mainboards and you begin to appreciate the fact that the term MPC has many different connotations.

The mainboard is an electronic assembly or PCB (Printed Circuit Board) that usually accommodates the processor, memory (Ram), Cache memory or static Ram, and expansion bus. It is the largest single electronic assembly in your MPC. The expansion bus permits the connection of subsystems such as hard disks, monitors, sound cards, video cards and CD-ROM drives. At present the most standard MPC bus is the ISA (Industry Standard Architecture) that was introduced by IBM through the launch of its 286-based PC AT computer. In 1987 IBM introduced the MCA (Micro Channel Architecture) bus through its PS/2 range of Personal Systems. Another bus type is EISA (Enhanced Industry Standard Architecture) which was developed and introduced by nine leading PC clone makers including Compaq.

Though both EISA and MCA are improvements on ISA, they still restrict the speed at which peripherals can be driven. For example, the clock speed of the bus does not match that of the processor's external bus. For example, even though the data bus might be running at 50 MHz, an ISA bus will run at around 10 MHz.

The commercially successful method of increasing bus performance is to use what is termed a local bus. This connects directly to the processor's external data bus and so yields a considerable improvement in data throughput when compared to that of an ISA bus. The performance of both local bus graphics and local bus hard disk controllers is superior to that of their ISA equivalents. VESA (Video Electronics Standards Association) Local Bus slots are the most widely used at present, though alternatives do exist, such as Intel's PCI Bus.

If you wish to take advantage of local bus ancillaries, you obviously need a mainboard fitted with appropriate local bus expansion slots. Also, any local bus cards you may buy must naturally comply with those on the mainboard.

Clock speed and processor type can be assumed to provide a *general* indication as to how fast a PC will be, there are many other contributory factors which influence machine performance. The operation of a computer depends upon the complex interaction between numerous devices and subsystems. A 40 MHz 386 machine, for example, fitted with a slow hard disk will prove particularly sluggish when running applications which require intensive read/write operations, such as databases or even Windows when insufficient memory has led to the inclusion of a swap file (virtual memory) on hard disk.

Some like to know just how many times faster a machine is than the original IBM 4.77 MHz 8088-based PC, using various utilities. But a more satisfactory test is where processing power is determined from several different angles. For example, processing speed can be measured in terms of Millions of Instructions Per Second (MIPS), Whetstones, and Dhrystones yielded. A Whetstone is a standard benchmark for measuring floating point computations – the binary equivalent of decimal arithmetic. A high rating naturally makes the machine suited to arithmetic intensive operations, such as computer graphics that depend upon matrix transformations. A Dhrystone test provides a guide to raw processing power, and for this reason is unsatisfactory used in isolation.

Performing such tests does not require a specialised laboratory testbed – a commercially available diagnostics program may be sufficient. One such program is CheckIt from TouchStone Software Corporation (Seal Beach, CA). More sophisticated programs include Ziff-Davis' PC Bench 7.x, which tests each and every aspect of a PC and is probably the most sophisticated bench test program in the world today. This produces overall results for processor, video, hard disk and memory based on a battery of detailed tests.

To determine the practical performance of a machine, however, comparative test running everyday programs are often more desirable. For example, how does the machine cope with ToolBook in the Windows environment? Or indeed, how does it run Windows in general? And what is it like running Microsoft Encarta or other MPC titles that you wish to use?

Ziff-Davis also publishes probably the world's leading test program for determining machine performance under Windows. Such tests as drawing dialogue boxes/sec, clearing screens, and drawing mixed fonts each combine to give an accurate appraisal of a PC's Windows performance.

The sophistication of Intel processors (used in IBM computers) is increasing steadily, and current high-end machines may well become entry level systems by the mid nineties. Intel, and numerous other deciding forces in the industry, claim that the next generation of software will be aimed at 486- and Intel Pentium-based machines. For example, Windows NT (New Technology) launched in mid 1993 requires a 486-compliant or Pentium processor. As Microsoft is a considerable force in computer software, significance can be attached to which machines are being targeted.

However, the coexistence of 386- and 486-based machines is a reasonably healthy one at present. For example, Microsoft Windows 3.1 launched in 1992 will even run on 286- and 386SX-based machines, and the MPC minimum specification still embodies a 386SX processor. Also, the latest version of IBM's operating system, initially launched to coincide with the introduction of the IBM PS/2 range in 1987, runs on 386SX machines. Like Windows NT, OS/2.1 is a 32-bit, multitasking operating system, and has a GUI in the form of its Presentation Manager.

If buying a 486 mainboard, it is advisable to choose a processor-upgradable variant that supports 486DX processors as well as the Pentium. And if you with to upgrade the system yourself, you should buy a mainboard fitted with ZIF (Zero Insertion Force) processor socket. This has a small lever, which when depressed permits you tc remove and to insert processors without the possibility of bending or even breaking the processor pins.

Note, while carrying out DIY on your MPC/PC unplug all power leads from the mains supply, and ensure that you wear a wrist-strap which can be used to earth your body and so eliminate the presence of electrostatic charges that can destroy CMOS electronic devices through the touch of a hand. You can obtain a wrist-strap from any electronics outlet.

That the processor unit of an MPC should be an IBM module or 100% compatible, is vitally important. The most obvious area in where incompatibility occurs between clones lies in the Basic Input Output System (BIOS). This is a piece of firmware (See Glossary) in that it is a machine-code program which resides in a Read Only Memory (ROM) variant.

Widely recognised 100% IBM compatible BIOS packages include American Megatrends Inc (AMI), Phoenix and Award chips. Problem or incompatible BIOS chips can often be exchanged for these. It should be said that all but a minute portion of IBM clones are compatible in terms of supporting PC peripheral devices and software.

3.3.2 Memory

The acceptable minimum of Random Access Memory (RAM), a rewritable form of electronic memory, is increasing as commercial programs become increasingly complex. All MPC titles require at least 2 Mbyte of RAM, with many publishers recommending at least 4 Mb. It is likely that we will see a continual rise in memory requirements. (Incidentally, RAM is something of a misnomer as Read Only Memory (ROM) also offers 'random access'.)

Initially there were a number of limiting factors that prevented the inclusion of large amounts of memory in a conventional PC design. The first and most obvious of these was the number of physical address lines on the processor itself. In brief, if an address bus is connected directly to memory, it is found that n address lines results in to 2^n memory addresses.

The now-defunct Intel 4004 processor, launched in 1971 at a development cost of $60,000, could access just 4 Kbytes of memory directly. The Intel 8088 processor launched in 1979 – upon which the IBM PC XT was based – had a 20-line address bus giving access to 2^{20} or 1,048,576 bytes (one Mbyte) of memory.

When in 1981 IBM launched the PC XT, the 640 Kbyte ceiling of user RAM was perceived as adequate. The remaining 360 Kbytes of one Mbyte addressable memory was given to system firmware.

To coincide with the need for increased RAM, and helped by falling RAM prices in the mid-eighties, Lotus, Intel and Microsoft collaborated in the development of LIM (Lotus Intel Microsoft) memory. This is commonly known as EMS (Expanded Memory System).

A more widely used alternative to expanded memory is the Extended Memory System (XMS), which is now more popular than EMS. It is usually possible to plug in around 32 Mbytes of extended memory directly into the motherboard of 386, 486 and Pentium based machines. Through the addition of a proprietary memory board some mainboards allow a further 32 Mbytes of RAM to be added.

Almost all desktop MPCs/PCs use 32-pin Simms (Serial In-line Memory Modules), which may be either 256 Kbytes, 1 Mbyte (most common), or 4 Mbytes. Also, almost all mainboards come with eight Simm sockets and support a number of different memory sizes. The number of memory sizes supported and the manner in which are they configured will be shown clearly in the mainboard manual. However, the following memory configurations can be assumed on all memory boards:

Memory size	*Configuration*
1 Mbyte	1 * 1 Mbyte Simm
2 Mbyte	2 * 1 Mbyte Simm
4 Mbyte	4 * 1 Mbyte Simm
8 Mbyte	8 * 1 Mbyte Simm

1 Mbyte Simms normally consist of nine memory chips, cheaper 3-chip solutions are available that are suitable for many systems. RAM speed is measured in nano seconds (ns) and typically varies from 100ns down to 50ns.

The second type of memory supported by many highly specified mainboards is called cache memory or the external cache. Its called the external cache because 486 processors have an internal cache on the processor chip itself.

Unlike system memory RAM, which is dynamic, the memory cache is static meaning that it is not refreshed periodically. It is therefore extremely fast and acts as an intermediate buffer between the processor and system ancillaries. Physically cache memory consists of DIP (Dual In-line packages) and most mainboards support up to 256 Kbytes or 512 Kbytes.

3.3.3 Graphic Controllers

The copious supply of graphic controllers and monitors for the PC are meshed by several industry standards. These include Monochrome Display Adapter (MDA), Colour Graphics Adapter (CGA), Enhanced Graphics Adapter (EGA), Video Graphics Array (VGA), Multi Colour Graphics Array (MCGA), 8514/A, Extended Graphics Adapter (XGA), as well as others. Like all add-ins for PCs, graphic controllers (adapter cards) plug directly into expansion slots. They may be either ISA, EISA, MCA or local bus.

Pixel resolutions delivered through industry standard controllers include 640-by-480, 800-by-600, 1024-by-768 and 1280-by-1024. Most VGA cards are able to switch between at least two modes of resolution. An enhanced VGA card, for example, may offer both 800-by-600 and 1024-by-768 pixels resolution modes, as well as others. True VGA implementations are able to emulate MDA, CGA and EGA modes of operation.

It is important to note that enhanced VGA implementations differ, and often require indigenous software drivers to run popular commercial software. High specification enhanced VGA cards fitted with 1 Mb VRAM can provide 256 colours at 1024-by-768 pixels. Variants that feature 65K colours are also commercially available, and controllers delivering 1280-by-1024 pixels resolution are becoming increasingly popular.

Refresh rate, the frequency at which screen images are redrawn, is also important. Interlaced graphics modes operate by separating screens into two fields. One field scans back and forth drawing odd lines while the other draws the even lines. This technique is used in broadcast television.

Initially, the critical advantage of interlacing *was* a reduction in screen flicker, and was originally introduced into broadcast television because scan rates were too slow to draw screens as one complete field.

Nowadays fast non-interlaced monitors generate the best images, and tend not to cause eye strain associated with old fashioned computer monitors. The refresh rates, measured in Hertz (Hz), should be such so as to avoid even invisible flicker, which is known to cause eye strain. Around 70 Hz (or higher) should be considered an adequate refresh rate.

High performance controllers for Windows are now available, and based on various chipsets. This include those based on the S3 chipset. However, the highest performance controllers are local bus variants, many of which (with 2 Mb video RAM) can drive monitors at a resolution of 1280*1024*65K colours.

Generally controllers that slot into a standard AT bus are greatly out-performed by modern local bus controllers. These bypass the slow AT bus and connect almost directly to the processor's data bus, and therefore run at a considerably higher frequency. Local bus controllers require appropriate slots, which cannot be assumed to exist in all mainboard designs. Local bus controllers include those based on the Tseng ET4000 chip and Cirrus chipset.

3.3.4 Monitors

Like graphic controllers, monitors vary a great deal in terms of technical specification. An appropriate marriage between monitor and controller is therefore essential. An optimum pairing is one in which both the specification of the monitor and controller are exploited fully.

Conventional colour displays based upon the ubiquitous Cathode Ray Tube (CRT) consist of a number of phosphor deposits (pixels) each consisting of red, blue and green phosphors. A 1024-by-768 pixel resolution monitor, for example, will comprise at least 786,432 deposits of red, green and blue phosphors. The phosphors (pixels) are normally arranged in a delta or star formation. An electron beam scans horizontal lines of pixels, exciting them to varying degrees thus giving luminance and chrominance. To help focus the electron beam, a fine mask is included which helps separate each pixel and so improve picture definition.

With a non-interlaced arrangement the maximum rate at which lines can be scanned or swept, is termed the horizontal scan rate (or horizontal frequency). After scanning all the horizontal rows, the electron beam moves diagonally to begin scanning once again. The maximum frequency at which all the horizontal lines are scanned is critical, and is termed the vertical scan rate, vertical frequency, or refresh rate).

It is essential to synchronise the scan rate with incoming signals. A multisync (or multifrequency) monitor can synchronise itself with various incoming signals. However, there are many implementations of the term 'multisync monitor', the simplest of which will automatically synchronise with perhaps two horizontal frequencies and maybe two or three vertical ones. In essence these are *dual frequency* monitors. (Incidentally, MultiSync is a registered trademark of NEC.)

Professional versions are able to synchronise with a range of horizontal and vertical frequencies. A *scanning range* determines the variety of acceptable signal sources.

The NEC MultiSync 3FG possesses a scan range which embodies all controllers from CGA up to 8514/A and XGA adapters. Such monitors are naturally flexible in terms of interchangeability between various systems, such as PCs and Macintosh computers.

Many monitors economise on scan range, thus concentrating on the narrow band of professional graphic controllers such as EGA and VGA. For example, the Panasonic PanaSync C1381 and C1381i. The pixel resolution achieved, is a function of both graphic controller and monitor, thus emphasising the importance of the coupling.

Monitor resolution largely depends upon pixel density, which is related to dot-pitch. Dot-pitch is the distance (from centre to centre) between pixels. On professional 14'' monitors this will be as low as .26 or .28 mm. On larger monitors (17'' or bigger), high resolutions can still be achieved, in spite of increased dot-pitch.

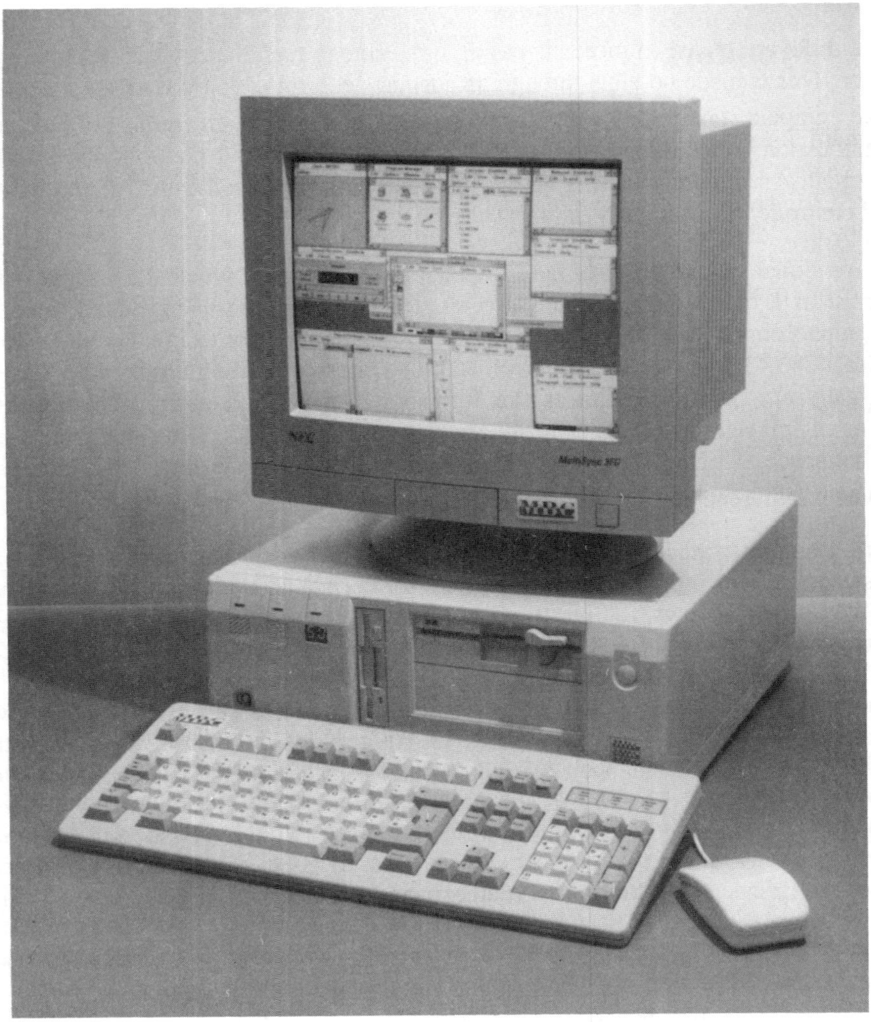

Fig 3.6: NEC MultiSync 3FG monitor

3.3.5 Magnetic Hard Disks

The usefulness of a stand-alone PC is greatly enhanced following the installation of a magnetic hard disk drive, which presents a practical solution to re-writable mass storage for the present. Hard disk data capacities have steadily increased since the 10 Mbyte disks (for the IBM PC XT) of the early eighties. It now looks certain that the nineties will see the widespread acceptance of disks in the hundreds of Mbytes and even Gigabyte range.

Smaller (30, 60 or 80 Mbyte) hard disks remain appropriate in many instances, however. These can provide a starting point for future expansion, where additional hard disks are added to meet increasing data storage requirements as and when they occur. This is made possible through an adequate controller and power supply.

All hard disks must be paired with an appropriate controller, with which they must be 100 percent compatible. Popular commercial variants include MFM, RLL, IDE, ESDI and SCSI. These are usually plug-in cards. Almost all controllers tend also to support floppy disk drives.

There are basically three ways in which a controller can be supported:

- It is included on the motherboard itself.
- Or, it is combined with a hard drive in the form of a hard card where the complete assembly is plugged into an expansion slot.
- Or, it represents a single card which plugs into an expansion slot.

Most single-card controllers are able to support at least two hard disks drives. In terms of future expansion, SCSI variants excel, where up to seven hard disks can often be connected. Depending upon the implementation, ESDI controllers usually accommodate up to four hard disks.

Controllers capable of accepting multiple devices provide an economical path to vast data storage capacity in future. An inexpensive array of drives can be built up, thus lowering the considerable cost of a single high capacity drive bought at the outset. Where a number of drives in an array exhibit comparatively lengthy access times, it may be more practical to replace them with a single large disk, or several larger ones.

More expensive controllers are often expandable in terms of additional daughter boards. For example, SCSI daughter boards can increase the number of drives in standard multiples of seven. Such controllers can easily yield tens of Gbytes using inexpensive drives. Some controllers are also capable of 'mirroring', i.e. writing the same data to two disk drives simultaneously, thus making the data more secure.

Controller technology and performance has advanced considerably in recent years, giving rise to an array of commercial devices ranging from scant MFM implementations to caching variants comprising on-board processors. The main thrust of advancement bases itself on the need to expand data capacities, lower access times, and increase data transfer rates. In addition, the emergence of multiple device controllers reveals a secondary aim. Inexpensive controllers depend upon a proprietary bus connection. Sophisticated versions include an on-board processor. High performance controllers can be separated into two groups: track-buffered and cache types. The most sophisticated are cache controllers which include on-board processors.

Cache controllers speed up read/write operations by using on-board RAM as an intermediate data store between disk and system memory. Based upon which data is requested most often, a caching algorithm estimates which portions of hard disk should reside in on-board RAM. The ingenuity of this technique simply takes advantage of the inescapable fact that a small percentage of disk data is rewritten and accessed most frequently. The decision making process regarding which data should reside in RAM fuels the view that they are 'intelligent controllers'.

Cache controllers are the most expensive of all variants, and will out-perform standard implementations. It is most often these types of controllers that are able to support increasing multiples of drives through the addition of daughter boards. High performance cache controllers can offer access times as low as a fraction of one ms.

The operation of track-buffered controllers is entirely different. A modest amount of on-board RAM (typically 32 – 64 Kbytes) is normally incorporated and are exceptionally low cost in comparison with cache controllers. They also support three floppy disk drives, as opposed to the two of most cache controllers.

Data capacity is a function of the drive mechanism and, to a lesser extent, of the manner in which it is formatted. Important factors which govern hard disk performance include data transfer rate and access time.

Average data transfer rates will be in the region of hundreds of Kbytes/sec. Using modest partnerships such as a 40 Mbyte drive and IDE controller, an average data transfer rate of about 450 Kbytes/sec is typical.

Data transfer rate is greatly increased using SCSI-2 compliant controllers, and to a lesser extent using SCSI-1 implementations. Local bus controllers are also available and these too greatly out-perform controllers such as conventional ISA IDE variants. Access time is the latency period between a data request and commencement of reading that data. Considerably shorter than on a CD-ROM drive, it typically ranges from 65 ms down to 13 ms on mainstream computers, with those systems fitted with cache controllers offering access times of a fraction of a millisecond. Physically, hard disks may be either 3.5'' or 5.25'' in diameter, and are usually non-removable.

Sharing the internal power supply unit (PSU), hard disks are often supported in frames at the front of the processor unit. They are connected to controllers via ribbon cable terminated with IDCs (Insulation Displacement Connectors).

External hard disks comprise independent PSUs and are more expensive than equivalent internal drives. These are normally used because of a shortage of drive bays or because of an insufficient power supply.

Compact enough to fit easily into a brief case, removable hard disks, separable from machine and controller, make programs and data exceptionally portable.

Hard cards, like conventional hard disks, are non-removable, and comprise a controller and hard disk as a single module. Their principal advantage is that of ease of installation. Disadvantages include: the controller is dedicated to just one drive, it will not support floppy disk drives, and it can consume a full expansion slot, often leaving only sufficient room for just a half card in an adjacent slot.

3.3.6 Motion Video

FMFSV (at 25-30 fps) requires an appropriate delivery board or decoder able to decompress images stored on CD-ROM or other DSM (See Section 3.1). A leading example is the Intel ActionMedia 750 Delivery Board available for PC ATs and PS/2s. It generates FMFSV at 25 frames/50 fields per second for PAL, or 30 frames/60 fields per second for NTSC (See Glossary).

Compatibility is essential where the method, by which motion video is encoded onto DSM (compression algorithm), does not conform to the MPEG or JPEG standards. Note, it is possible to generate motion video using the JPEG algorithm even though it is intended for still-image compression.

3.3.7 Intel Digital Video Interactive – Overview

Digital Video Interactive (DVI) was demonstrated at the second Microsoft CD-ROM conference of 1987. An image-compression technology, DVI permits FMFSV in the PC environment.

DVI currently consists of two boards. The ActionMedia 750 Delivery Board decompresses data, and the ActionMedia 750 Capture Board captures and compresses that data. The Delivery Board alone is required for multimedia delivery. DVI offers numerous features essential for acceptable multimedia. Video can be merged with VGA text and graphics where a window showing motion video can be combined. High quality audio can be delivered concurrently with motion video. Full-colour, FMFSV at 10 to 30 fps is displayed at 512-by-480 pixel resolution.

3.3.8 DVI ActionMedia 750 Delivery Board

The ActionMedia 750 Delivery Board provides a means of video and audio playback in a PC AT or PS/2 environment. Two boards are available that are specific to either PC AT or PS/2.

Frame rate and pixel resolution of FMFSV can equate to 30 and 512 by 480 pixels, respectively. Seventy-two minutes of such video can be reaped from a single DVI CD-ROM disc. Longer playing discs are possible by sacrificing resolution, frame-rate, screen-size or image quality during development.

Video stills can also be delivered at various pixel resolutions. Lower screen resolutions and higher compression ratios yield more compact image data, thus enabling a greater number of video stills.

Provided the resultant quality is acceptable, up to 80,000 images can be stored on a single disc, opening up the possibility of profusely illustrated material in single-disc operation. The board is also able to deliver varying qualities of mono or stereo audio with motion video concurrently.

3.3.9 DVI ActionMedia 750 Delivery Board – Technical Overview

With either one or two Mbytes of video RAM (VRAM), the ActionMedia 750 Delivery Board decompresses image and audio data laid using the Intel ActionMedia 750 Capture Board (See Chapter 4). Real-time decompression takes place via an on-board SCSI controller. Appropriate cable attachments for both internal (50-pin) and external (38-pin) SCSI devices are included.

DVI is currently implemented using the i750 chip set, which includes the 82750PA and the 82750DA. The former is a pixel processor which draws and manipulates bitmaps in VRAM, while the latter simultaneously writes previously written/ manipulated bitmaps to screen.

Both chips combine to give a performance of 75,000 (8 by 10) characters/sec, or 3000 flat or solid (8-bit 1000 pixel) polygons per second. These figures become meaningful when considering that a typical 16-bit VGA card delivers around 5000 characters/sec. The pixel processor yields 12.5 million pixel operations per second.

Full-colour, full-screen motion video is displayed at 30 fps from CD-ROM, hard disk, other SCSI storage device, RAM or digital network. A 512-by-480 pixel resolution is generated from 256 by 240 pixel bitmaps in VRAM. A standard 15-pin 'D' type connector is included for a VGA or multisync monitor. The AT version has a digital display connector in the form of a 40 pin YUV output.

Stereo or mono output is supported using a 32 MHz digital signal processor. Four streams of audio are mixed down to two output channels giving a maximum frequency response of 16 KHz over an 84 dB dynamic range. Audio playback can be modified in terms of sampling rate and filtering levels. An audio only output is ported via the external SCSI port.

At present, the underlying i750 chipset is a quintessential first step, and will provide the momentum required toward achieving greater power and flexibility. An imminent second generation is poised to make the video processor twice as powerful. A third generation is foreseen to be five times more powerful again. Intel envisages DVI integrated onto chips which plug directly into the motherboard. Intel also claims that it will integrate the whole of DVI into the microprocessor architecture itself – though this seems an extremely long-term forecast.

3.3.10 Windows Multimedia Extensions

The sheer size of the PC installed user base brings with it a potentially large market for PC multimedia products, and falling PC CD-ROM drive prices do a great deal to speed up its arrival. Both the Multimedia PC and the Windows multimedia extensions that form part of Windows 3.x (See Fig. 3.7) will also hasten the arrival of this market.

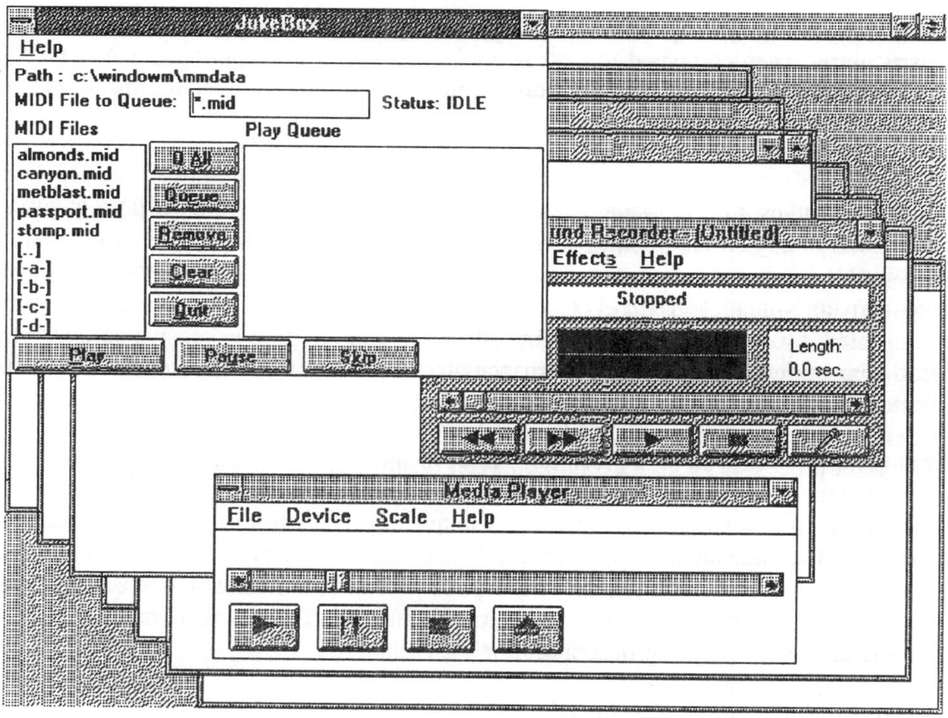

Fig 3.7: Windows 3.1 Multimedia screen

Microsoft Windows (a multi-tasking environment) has achieved a level of success which now makes it a reasonably common PC environment. Indeed a growing number of mainstream applications now require Windows to run, and we can now see Modular Windows appear in such multimedia appliances is the Tandy VIS. Modular Windows is Microsoft's attempt to widen the Windows user-base to embody consumer appliances. For example, in future you may well see HDTVs, VCRs and other domestic appliances come with Modular Windows rather than a cryptic set of buttons.

The multimedia extensions are an attempt to introduce a common environment for PC multimedia delivery, yielding a degree of compatibility which has evaded the PC thus far. It is hoped that they will convert much of the growing Windows user base to being a significant PC multimedia user base. The Extensions provide control over typical multimedia peripheral devices such as CD-ROM drives, and make the integration of image files, MIDI files and audio (or WAV) files possible.

3.3.1 Sound cards

The primitive sound capability of a standard PC or PS/2 is a significant disadvantage, particularly when compared to that of machines such as the Commodore Amiga. For this reason the MPC (level 1) specification includes an 8-bit sound card, though a 16-bit variant is preferred.

With suitable software, sound cards can be used for such purposes as sampling, playing synthesized polyphonic sequences, speech synthesis and as MIDIs (Musical Instrument Digital Interfaces). The latter application, however, often requires additional hardware which can usually be assumed to be a MIDI connector box or similar, to which MIDI keyboards and other compatible devices can then be connected. Most cards also operate in full stereo, and on more expensive variants you can expect features such as reverb thus giving multimedia developers ability to emulate various acoustic conditions.

Sampling permits you to digitise and store, in memory or on disk, live sounds from an analogue source. For example, it is possible to sample a short sequence from a CD player, using a microphone or the direct output from a player's headphone socket or that which is connected to an amplifier. The duration of sequences is often restricted by memory capacity, and overall sound quality of different cards varies according to individual specification. Occasionally, sampled sequences can be compressed by a modest degree thus saving disk space.

Popular 8-bit sound cards include Ad Lib and SoundBlaster Pro (from Creative Technology, which has built-in MIDI support and Ad Lib emulation). Both cards offer 11 FM (Frequency Modulated) synthesized voices. Other sound cards include the Turtle Beach MultiSound, SoundBlaster 16 ASP, MediaVision Pro Audio Spectrum, Roland LAPC1, Ad Lib GOLD, and Microsoft Windows Sound System.

3.3.2 Microsoft Video for Windows

Microsoft Video for Windows (VfW) is a response to Apple QuickTime, which has quickly become a de facto software standard for producing motion video in the

Macintosh environment. VfW permits video playback, capture and editing. Minimum PC requirements is an MPC specified machine. A 486-based MPC can yield near FMPSV covering quarter of the screen and running at 25 fps. With a video delivery device fitted, such as those based upon the Intel i750 chipset, video running at up to 30 fps is possible.

Video clips can be added to applications through OLE (Object Linking and Embedding). For example, video clips can be added to Lotus Ami Pro, MS Word, MS Excel, Lotus Notes, and a growing number of others.

Video capture requires an appropriate video capture board and 30 MHz 386-based system. Also included is a means of converting QuickTime into the VfW format. VfW supports the AVI (Audio Video Interleaved) format and has an installable Codec interface.

3.4 IBM Multimedia

IBM offers an array of hardware and software products facilitating multimedia delivery and development, ranging from the low-cost *LinkWay Live!*, ActionMedia (DVI) to its Ultimedia range of systems and OS/2 2.1 operating system that features multimedia extensions.

1991 marked something of a turning point for IBM, as the nature of multimedia opened up new markets for it. Education, TV programme and film makers, designers and retailers are several new groupings targeted. The existing business and corporate client base was also be stimulated, where it can be argued that multimedia is of equal, if not more, importance.

The impact of multimedia upon business computing is becoming clearer now that the surrounding technology matures, and so the transition from visualised concepts to 'real-world implementations' gets under way. Image databases, for example, represents just one of applications yielded by multimedia technology.

Clearly the role of what might be called a business machine is to be altered: no longer solely confined to word processor, spreadsheet, database, accounts and communications applications, the business computer is just as likely to be adorned by photographic images and video.

We have to discriminate between multimedia technology and the multimedia concept: for example an image database, though it might use advanced relational database techniques is not strictly multimedia. Video telecommunications is another example of what multimedia is not, though the vehicle will be provided by multimedia technology producing the appropriate environment. As it so happens video telecommunications is an important aspect of this new technology, and it is without doubt that employees in corporations, other enterprises and institutions will become used to communicating through this perhaps unnerving technique. Indeed it is this technology which will become notable catalytic influence in the growing exodus of workers from the work place to the home; 'home workers' are now performing many of the tasks previously possible only at the work place.

3.4.1 LinkWay Live!

A software product developed for the education sector, LinkWay Live! provides a low-cost hypertext orientated authoring and delivery environment which can be used to combine audio, visual and textual material. With links between relevant information implanted, point-and-click buttons on screen, and pop-up information panels (which can be links leading to further panels), applications can provide reasonably effective educational presentations or CAL.

With a high profile in schools, LinkWay Live! receives much support, interest and in some respects can be considered a de facto standard for 'hypertext' courseware. Third party support exists in the form of clip-art, clip-animation, clip-sound effects which can assist low-budget applications at schools, colleges, universities and even in the corporate and industry sectors. Complete LinkWay Live! applications are available, made easy by IBM permitting free distribution of run-time versions of applications. Applications can be run on either stand-alone systems or LANs, where the latter requires an IBM Authenticity to Copy (ATC) licence for every student workstation.

Despite being initially developed for the education market, LinkWay Live! has been, and continues to be, exploited as a professional authoring tool for in-house and commercial CD-ROM titles. For example, The Software Toolworks Encyclopedia of Mammals, was developed in conjunction with IBM using *LinkWay Live!*. The product is described as multimedia, providing textual information, animal vocalisations and animations. The animations are relatively crude but effective sequences of video stills confined to approximately one quarter of the screen, loaded from CD-ROM into memory before playback.

It should be said that, technically, LinkWay Live! is not a hypertext authoring tool, as wrongly described, but a hypermedia authoring tool as it can exploit graphics, video stills, animations and so forth, meshed by meaningful paths defined through user-interaction. LinkWay Live! can also be used to access audio, speech, CD-ROM and video disc material following installation of appropriate adapter cards.

Linkway runs on any IBM PC or PS/2 computer with a mouse and at least 384 Kbytes of RAM, and a colour CGA, EGA, MCGA or VGA monitor; and a hard disk is recommended. IBM PC DOS 2.1 or higher is also needed. Note, these requirements are not relevant to applications embodying motion video.

For developers and users that require a little more than LinkWay Live!, there is IBM StoryBoard Live which is aimed at, though not exclusively used, those wishing to develop multimedia presentations. Like LinkWay Live!, hardware requirements are minimal, necessitating an IBM PC or PS/2 together with EGA or VGA graphics controller and display. Note, once again these requirements are not relevant to applications embodying motion video.

Both LinkWay Live! and StoryBoard Live can be used in conjunction with the IBM M-Motion Video Adapter/A which provides full-motion, full colour video, and is specific to the PS/2 family of computers.

3.4.2 Audio Visual Connection

IBM Audio Visual Connection (AVC) is a high-end multimedia authoring (software) system able to combine high quality stereo sound together with full-motion video. Specific to the PS/2 family of computers, AVC is able to exploit analogue motion video emanating from numerous sources, such as video cameras, videodisc closed circuit cameras and VCRs.

The successful delivery of full motion analogue video and high quality sound within multimedia created using AVC requires the following system components:

- IBM PS/2 or MCA compatible – models 50, 55SX, 60, 65, 70 or 80;
- Hard disk (typically 100 Mbytes or larger);
- M-Motion Video Adapter/A which digitises analogue video and writes it to hard disk before playback, also reproduces AM quality sound;
- Videodisc player;
- AVC Audio Capture and Playback adapter;
- IBM compatible Mouse;
- 3.5'' floppy disk drive;
- IBM 8512, 8513, 8514, 8515 monitor, permitting the display of all VGA modes;
- DOS 3.3 or better

or,

- OS/2 or Microsoft Windows.

3.4.3 PS/2 Ultimedia

1992 saw the launch of the IBM Ultimedia range of systems based on the PS/2 range of computers. They each include CD-ROM XA drives and now (1993) include OS/2 2.x, DOS and Windows 3.1 pre-installed. They are configured as dual-boot systems where the user has the option of loading the required operating system environment.

The PS/2 Ultimedia M57 and M77 represent the two basic configurations. Each has a 16-bit stereo sound subsystem (M-Audio Adapter/A), 8 Mb Ram and a 212 Mb hard disk with a 12 ms average access time.

3.4.4 OS/2 2.1

The release of OS/2 2.1 in mid-1993 saw the inclusion of multimedia extensions, which compare with those of Windows. Referred to as Multimedia Presentation Manager/2 (MMPM/2). It supports standard multimedia devices including audio CD and videodisc control. Pre-release copies of the extensions also featured CD-ROM XA support.

Features include a media player, volume control and data convertor. The latter can be used to convert audio and graphics files created using IBM's Audio Visual Connection (AVC) into OS/2's MMPM/2 format.

3.5 Tandy VIS and Modular Windows

The Tandy VIS is probably the most standard, but not the most advanced, of all the currently available multimedia appliances. Its most standard features concern the fact that it is MPC/Windows compliant. Tandy has achieved this compatibility by adopting Modular Windows as the UI/OS and basing the design on a 286 processor. Theoretically, MPC titles can be freely ported over to VIS, and the process of developing VIS titles will involve tools with which a large percentage of developers are more than familiar. Both Owl International and AimTech have announced VIS authoring tools.

Current VIS implementations have a standard CD-ROM drive and controller partnership that is incapable of reading with single- session or multi-session PhotoCDs. However, the VIS is an open architecture, and because it relies upon many of the facets that make up what can be termed a standard PC. For example, future VIS systems can include faster processors and later versions of Modular Windows that support the many MPC titles. Current VIS appliances have incorporate sockets for video accelerator and a modem.

3.6 Portable Multimedia Systems

1992 saw the launch of two very different multimedia systems from two major players: the Philips CDI 360 and the Sony MMCD. With a US price tag of about $2000 the more sophisticated CDI 360 is currently twice as expensive as the MMCD.

The CDI 360 is a standard CDI system based on a Motorola 68000 processor and the OS/9 operating system. It has both NTSC and PAL outputs as well as its own 6 inch active-matrix colour display, able to produce 756 by 556 pixel resolution images. As is the case with non-portable CDI players, it supports full motion video through hardware.

The less expensive MMCD has a rather traditional 8086 processor and uses the most world's most popular operating system, DOS. The US version has no PAL output, but only an NTSC output. A 300 by 200 pixel resolution display is included. (Initial versions are devoid of a PAL output as well as a hardware solution to produce full motion video. The MMCD uses the CD-ROM XA disc format.

4.

Authoring

"I would predict by the early Nineties that this [multimedia] will become a universally accepted method of communication..." – Robert Abel

This chapter addresses the basic issues concerning the hardware and software requirements of a typical MPC authoring station. The processes involved in multimedia authoring and production are addressed also.

Any MPC consisting of the hardware and software components discussed in chapter 3 can be upgraded to an authoring station. The term *MPC authoring station*, however, has two very different meanings. It can refer explicitly to the basic hardware and software through which it is possible to develop multimedia with FMFSV and audio (See Fig. 4.1), or it can refer to a perfectly ordinary MPC used to support an authoring tool (or authoring system) such as Asymetrix ToolBook or similar. A widely used authoring system, ToolBook was used to create Microsoft Multimedia Beethoven: *The Ninth Symphony* (See Fig. 4.2).

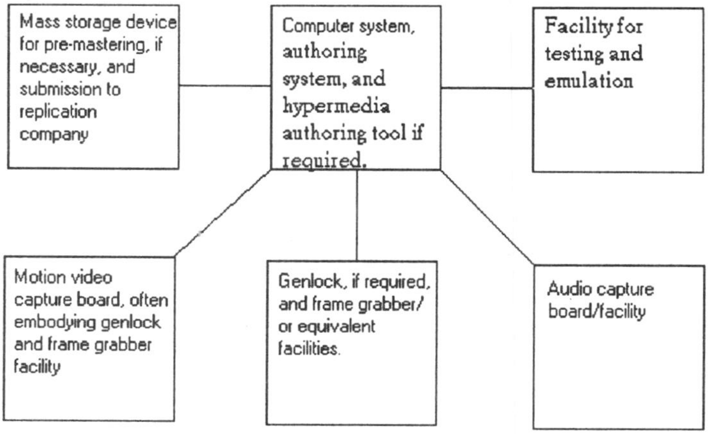

Fig. 4.1

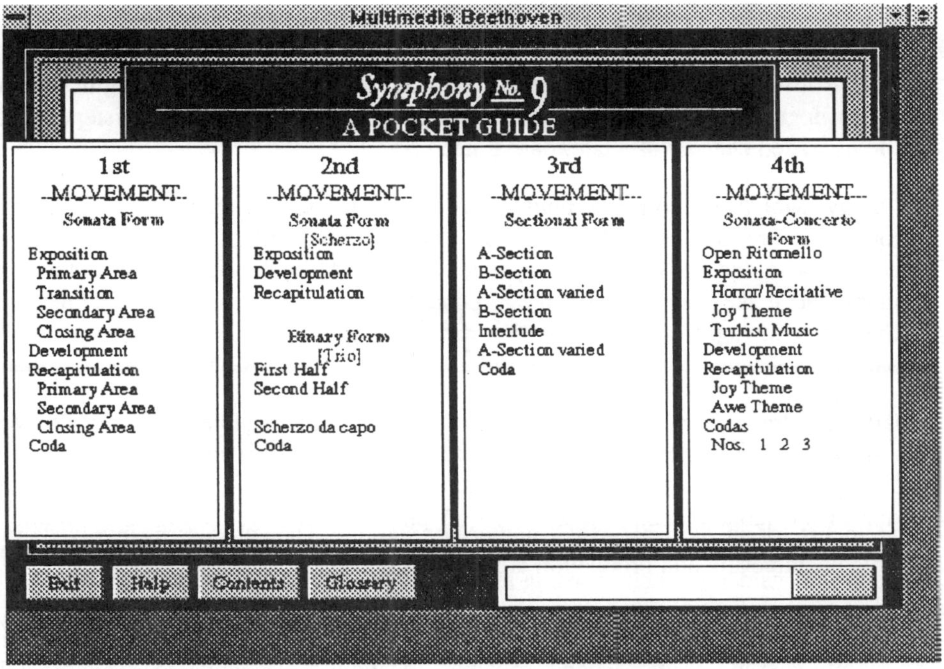

Fig. 4.2: Microsoft Multimedia Beethoven: The Ninth Symphony

Where such stations are required to produce multimedia for distribution on CD-ROM it is necessary to include a sufficiently large hard disk (or other random access digital storage device). This permits simulation and testing and, if required, it can be used to submit the final data to a replication company. This final stage can also be achieved through other media.

The hard disk data capacity required depends upon the volume of multimedia material to be developed. Often, a hard disk equal in data capacity to that of a CD-ROM disc is unnecessary because many applications might occupy only a small percentage of available CD data storage capacity.

Generally the issues and technical details discussed in chapter 3 for an MPC delivery system are equally valid when developing an MPC authoring station. You hear of people that have produced sophisticated multimedia presentations and even commercial MPC titles using little more than a base specification MPC.

In reality you will find that such a system will be under-powered in processor terms, have inadequate memory, and have insufficient hard disk space. Video recorders such as Intel's i750-based Smart Video Recorder and many others simply won't run on a system with 2 Mb RAM. Also, because of the large amount of disk space required to store video, a 30 Mb hard disk even if you double it using MS-DOS 6.0's DoubleSpace or other real-time disk compression utility, will be inadequate.

You really do need a reasonably high PC specification in order to produce sophisticated multimedia. But if you are a lone developer/producer don't leap in and buy the Rolls-Royce of MPC authoring stations. It may be better to begin with a processor upgradable 486/Pentium mainboard with some inexpensive subsystems, that can be upgraded cheaply at a later date if need be.

For many publishers, software houses and large multimedia producers, authoring station costs are less important and are usually academic. They will be more concerned with the person-hours expended, and will require fast MPC authoring stations that make best use of the producers and developers time. Savings in purchasing a low-spec authoring station are quickly eroded when labour costs are considered.

Equally, the cost of delivery systems must be considered, together with any licence fees (payable to the publishers of either retrieval systems or authoring programs) required to distribute applications. Licensing terms and conditions vary from one vendor to the next. Often, a licence can be purchased which permits an unlimited number of applications to be installed. Where relevant it is imperative that such matters are considered when choosing an appropriate authoring system.

Additional costs may emerge as a result of purchasing reproduction rights for copyright material, or/and paying royalties to individuals/companies. Almost all conventionally marketed and sold software, music, intellectual material, graphics, video and film is copyright protected. Without the publishers/owners permission you may not include such material in an MPC title for resale.

4.1 Video

Growth in electronic memory capacities, advancements in computer graphics, increased processing speeds, and better image compression techniques make digital video an increasingly logical choice. That this change should occur is a necessary precondition for the proliferation of reasonably sophisticated multimedia. In fact, PC multimedia really cam about as a result of digital video.

There are several techniques through which video can be integrated into a multimedia application, most of which can be achieved using relatively inexpensive equipment. Exact costs largely depend the video quality required, which include:

- Still digital video;
- Full-motion, part-screen digital video (FMPSV);
- Part-motion, part-screen digital video (PMPSV);
- Full-motion, full-screen digital video (FMFSV);

- Part-motion, full-screen digital video (PMFSV);
- Analogue video still (source);
- Full-screen, full-motion analogue video (source);
- Part-screen, full-motion analogue video (source).

Still digital video can be achieved using relatively low-cost frame grabbers, which take the form of plug-in expansion cards, and are able to digitise single frames of motion video. Many video recorders have a built-in frame grabbing feature.

Frames are naturally acquired in *1/(frame rate)* seconds or less: 1/25 sec for PAL and 1/30 seconds for NTSC. The longer the frame acquisition period, the lower the image definition achieved. The resultant quality also depends upon the video source material and hardware. For example, a good freeze frame facility can improve matters.

More similar to animations, motion video sequences constructed using a frame grabber can prove time consuming to produce, because each frame has to be painstakingly grabbed and added to a series of images that form a sequence.

A more effective method of producing part-motion video is to use a video recorder. Inexpensive versions, which work with VfW, include VideoBlaster, VideoSpygot, AITech's Video Surge, New Media Graphics Super VideoWindows and Matrox Marvel. Generally the frame rate at which these can capture video depends upon the complexity of graphics settings and video window size.

Analogue video, a standard method of storing video, (i.e. VHS), is obtainable through numerous sources such as Camcorders and VCRs. It must be stored on an external storage device such as videodisc player, or video tape, and for real-time applications, a video camera is used.

Most often, analogue video is stored on videodisc for the benefit of short access times. That all delivery systems must incorporate a videodisc player and video card thereafter can be regarded as a significant disadvantage. Videodisc players can be controlled using many authoring systems/tools (IBM AVC, TenCORE and Quest, for example) where (CAV) access times will be around three seconds or less.

4.1.1 Digital Video Interactive

The addition of an ActionMedia 750 Capture Board gives a complete Digital Video Interactive (DVI) authoring station. Like the delivery board, the capture board exists in two forms, specific either to the MCA (PS/2) or AT bus.

The capture board can simultaneously digitise audio and video, compressing both in real-time, making the overall station useful for applications outside multimedia such as traffic monitoring, video-teleconferencing, and many other situations which require remote viewing and recording.

Audio is captured using 14 bits per sample, and is compressed in real-time using an Adaptive Delta Pulse Code Modulation (ADPCM) software algorithm. Using Real-Time Video (RTV) software, video can be captured, compressed and delivered from 10 to 30 fps.

A still image capture facility is built-in, giving up to 1024 by 480 pixels resolution. Using appropriate software tools, varying degrees of image compression are possible where file size relates to quality achieved. (Note, applications which require real-time video capture necessitate both ActionMedia boards for successful delivery.)

4.1.2 IBM M-Motion Video Adapter/A

The IBM M-Motion Video Adapter/A is specific to the MCA bus, requiring an IBM PS/2 (model 50, 55SX, 60, 65, 70 or 80) or compatible with a 3.5'' disk drive. Occupying a single expansion slot, it consists of two boards sandwiched together. Output is compatible with all PS/2 monitors.

This is an entirely different technical approach to multimedia than DVI, with the emphasis placed upon controlling analogue source devices, as opposed to the achievement of high compression ratios for storing digital video and audio.

Through appropriate authoring software (AVC and Quest, for example), multimedia applications are able to reap analogue video and audio signals from videodisc for subsequent delivery. Both delivery and authoring stations must therefore comprise video adapters. Three NTSC or PAL inputs, or two Super VHS inputs can be harnessed under software control. Full-motion video and overlays are possible in all VGA modes with a maximum resolution of 640 by 480.

4.2 Still Images

Photographs and illustrations can be digitised using either a scanner, a still video camera, a PhotoCD, or a digital camera. Sub $1,000 digital cameras such as Canon's Xapshot and Logitech's Fotoman can sometimes be used. However, some have compared the resultant image quality of such cameras with that of a still frame from a consumer Camcorder – though that is not to rule them out if you have a rather tight budget.

4.2.1 Scanners – Images and Text

Scanners are used widely, and with appropriate software they permit the conversion of text into computer readable form. Investment in sophisticated scanning and camera equipment can be avoided where, perhaps, few images are required and a studio or even replication company can provide necessary services at competitive rates.Photographs and illustrations can be digitised using either an inexpensive hand-held scanner or a flat-bed scanner, of which full colour variants are commercially available.

Flat-bed scanners allow complete A4 or A3 pages to be scanned, and are ideal for digitising existing manuscripts, together with illustrations. If digitisation of a significant amount of material forms part of development, then a flat-bed scanner is essential. A fundamental advantage of flat-bed scanners is ease of use; when operated like a photocopier, high throughput can be achieved. Conversion of text into ASCII format requires optical character recognition (OCR) software.

Currently available hand-held scanners are often less sophisticated and much more difficult to use, requiring the user to pass the actual device over material while keeping it parallel with the paper's upper edge. In addition, usually only a small scanning width is achieved during a single pass. Many hand-held scanners are less than five inches wide. Though possible to build up images of A4 sheets through several scans, it is an extremely labour-intensive process. However, one or two A4 hand-held scanners are commercially available.

Hand-held scanners should only be chosen if it is necessary to digitise a modest quantity of relatively small photographs or illustrations (passport photographs, for instance). Where it is necessary to convert complete text pages into ASCII, a flat-bed scanner is required.

Scanning software will typically support a number of image file formats, such as TIFF, PCX, PIC and IMG. It will also support a number of features including windows to overlay one image on top of another, image inversion, rotation, paint editing, copy, paste and so on. Other features found in paint packages may also be available.

If further editing and manipulation is required, scanned images can be loaded into 'paint' programs such as Corel Draw, PC Paint, Gem Paint, Windows Paintbrush or similar. Often you can edit and manipulate images after loading them into an authoring system. For example, both IBM AVC and Quest permit this.

Modern flat-bed scanners can offer scanning resolutions up to 600 dots per inch (dpi), while hand-held scanners typically offer up to 400 dpi. Resolutions are likely to improve in the future.

4.2.2 Still Video Cameras

Effective digitisation of colour photographic images (slides or prints) or illustrations can also be achieved using a still video camera (SVC). This operates by writing images in analogue form to a two-inch diameter magnetic, (video) floppy disc that can store up to 50 exposures. (At Photokina in 1992 Canon demonstrated a digital camera which used a 2.5 inch hard disk to store up to 256 high-resolution images.)

The camera itself can be supported using a conventional tripod or vertical copy stand. With the latter, the camera lens points downward, making the process of aligning subject material and camera considerably easier. (Note, copying slides requires an appropriate photo stand adapter.)

Commercial SVCs often come with built-in flash, but extra, or alternative, lighting equipment is naturally required when copying photographs and illustrations. The disadvantage of SVCs is that the end result is a video frame composed of either 525 or 625 lines.

The first SVCs were launched in Japan in 1988 by Canon, Sony, Olympus and Pentax. The electonics and photographic company, Canon, launch the RC-251 Ion (Image On-line Network) in 1989. They followed this up with the RC-260 in 1991. Canon has since become a great believer in both SVC and so-called ESP (Electronic Still Presentation) systems. The latter is considered by Canon as the use of SVCs with computers in order to produce multimedia presentations. In 1991 Canon launched the Ion-PC kit for PC/AT compatibles and the Ion-Mac for the RC-260.

Professional SVCs tend to be expensive (in the $10,000 bracket). One such example is the Sony ProMavica MVC-7000, which produces high quality images.

4.2.3 Digital Cameras

Gaining better picture quality than that yielded by video cameras can be achieved using either a conventional camera or a sophisticated digital camera. Using a conventional 35mm, medium or even large format camera, processed photographs can either be scanned in the normal way, or processed onto PhotoCD. Using appropriate software, PhotoCD images can simply be converted into an appropriate image file format.

There are several sub $1,000 dollar digital cameras on the market including Logitech's Fotoman and Sony's Xapshot. But for professional usage, such variants as the Kodak DCS 200ci which costs around $25,000 dollars. The camera itself is a converted version of the famous Nikon F3. Instead of a film, it has a 1524 by 1012 pixel resolution CCD (charged coupled device) array, which produces sharp images of the same resolution. Using a SCSI cable it can be connected to either a PC or Mac that has a Future Domain 1660 SCSI controller.

4.3 The Authoring Process

"It is a standard, it's our standard..." – Sir Clive Sinclair

Such is the diversity of available media types within a true multimedia authoring environment, designers are able to work in a unique medium and call upon an array of skills, ranging from video editing to computer programming.

The multimedia producer/developer is difficult to define therefore: they may be an individual with creative flair and little or no programming skills, or a more technical individual with roots firmly entrenched in computer programming. It is probably true to say, however, that the of future multimedia will lie in the hands of creative individuals.

Varying career backgrounds of individuals making up design teams, gives a new and refreshing dimension to the general term 'developer', and dilutes the technical bias associated with the fraternity actively engaged in creating applications for computers and technology in general.

Multimedia development brings with it a great deal of responsibility, particularly where a commercial title may exist in the market for many years. Already we see titles where testing has obviously failed, and those which lack imagination or simply fail to harness the multimedia concept.

In fact the commercial success of specific multimedia delivery systems owes more to imaginative and technically competent designers and developers than to the technologies themselves. How big a success multimedia will be in future is linked to the quality, size and accessibility of the overall title base. In this respect it is hoped that the technology will become transparent, like a VCR for instance, where all that will matter are the multimedia titles themselves.

The challenge now is to develop titles which push the multimedia concept forward, while unveiling usage beyond the boundaries of linear media. It must be stressed, however, that multimedia can be defined in different years as a function of the technology of the day, but in reality multimedia is a philosophy which cannot be confined to any single technology at any one moment in time. It is a dynamic ever-expanding concept with which the designer and developer must grow in parallel, always seeking to re-evaluate theories and not be afraid to throw caution to the wind, and disagree with the kind of 'current thinking' or habit which often stifles new ideas and techniques.

4.4 Markets

In the sometimes harsh commercial landscape, realisation of a multimedia title requires the implementation of stages quite outside the often mechanised steps forming the development process itself (See Fig. 4.3). The size of the installed user base of the target system, demographic break down of the user base, the competing titles, are some of many staple considerations which need to be addressed.

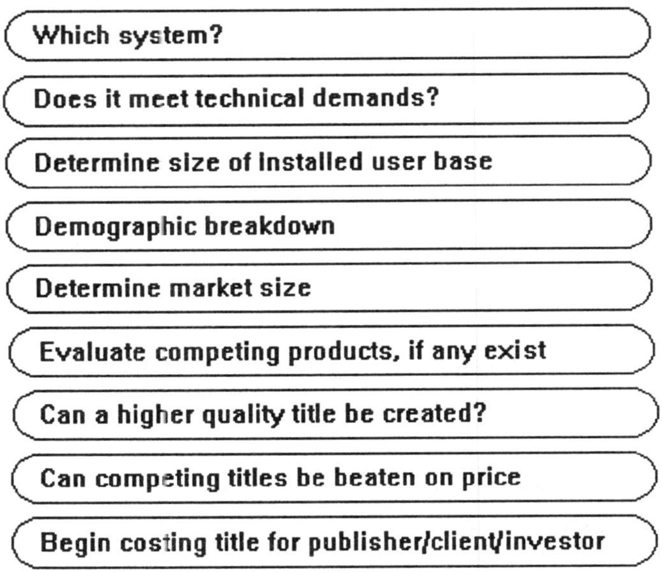

Fig. 4.3: steps in the development process

Until all multimedia delivery systems are encompassed by a standard interchangeable distribution medium and share common delivery capabilities, the question as to which system variant should be targeted is an inescapable one.

The system or systems chosen can influence the budget required, which in turn influences product pricing. Technical excellence and scale of production can also be functions of delivery system variant(s) chosen.

Driven partially by budget, product pricing hinges upon what the market can reasonably withstand. An original title, or one aimed squarely at a vertical market with few or no competing titles will often wield a high market value. However, originality can soon erode with the emergence of competing titles, as vertical markets can go horizontal all too quickly – multimedia itself epitomises such an evolutionary course.

The significance of being first in a new market is therefore obvious, giving licence to dictate product pricing, and thus optimise profits in the early stages. Sketching the learning curves of most commercially successful new products, it is found that an initially high product price plays an important future role in providing a price reduction capacity to compete with emerging (and possibly mimicking) products.

That the quality of any multimedia title is as high as possible is, of course, imperative, but this will do little to overcome problems such as: insufficient size of installed user base able to run title; over-priced product; and, more established competing titles.

The concept of commercially established, or what can be loosely regarded as standard titles, is something anyone who has grown up in the software industry will be more than aware of. It is a fact that users tend to cling to a program they first learned and, therefore, feel comfortable with. Regarded as industry standard programs, numerous word processors, spreadsheets and databases flourish upon user bases within which few members will even *try* alternative packages.

In many instances, multimedia titles will be no different. And like the software industry, companies will release clones while recognising possible legal consequences. Evidently, publishers have to take a number of rather delicate decisions, many of which are based on sketchy evidence, or simply trust in colleagues. Drawing upon expertise and experience of the design team is essential in this objective decision-making process.

Clearly, multimedia shares many of the self-same commercial considerations associated with any other industry. It is, however, a young one, and though the greatest opportunities will be offered in the early years, it will remain young enough and progressive enough to sustain new publishing opportunities for some time.

4.5 User Base

The decision as to which delivery system should be targeted can be a difficult one to make. Echoes of the rather non-standard computer industry reverberate, when software houses often gambled on the success of new machines.

However, software houses often made significant profits through successful but by no means standard machines. The games industry epitomises this. Both the Atari ST and Commodore Amiga cannot be considered standard machines, but each generates its own significant market.

The ensuing considerations represent the bulk of influential factors and questions which need to be weighed and answered while deciding which delivery system should be targeted:

Current size of installed user base;
- If small, is it likely to grow at the required rate over a given period?

Technical evaluation;
- Does technology meet technical demands of title?

Demographic breakdown;
- What portion of installed user base falls in target age group of title?

Evaluate existing competition specific (or otherwise) to user base:
- Do competing titles already exist?
- Can a better title be developed, and marketed and sold at a competitive price?

Determine authoring station and software costs if not installed:

Estimate cost of conversion to other multimedia delivery systems:

Ease of development:
- How well served in terms of authoring software?
- What level of support can be expected from vendors, and what services can they offer?
- What level of productivity can be expected from the accessible authoring station?
- Are members of existing design team familiar with authoring software and system?
- In terms of person-hours required for production and development, how does it compare with competing technologies?
- How many accessible studios specialise in chosen technology?

4.6 Costing

Negotiations with a publisher, or perhaps corporate client with regard to budget required, have to hinge on the reasonably accurate costing of development, which can naturally vary from one technology to another, and from one title to the next. For example, a considerable cost difference separates CDTV from CDI. Equally titles dependent upon a greater portion of original art-work and motion video can also prove costly.

The many variables involved and the early stage at which such costing must sometimes occur, means that estimations are often necessary.

The numerous staple stages which must be considered include:

- Multimedia authoring station (if not installed);
- Multimedia delivery systems (if not installed);

- Multimedia periphery devices (if not installed);
- Authoring software (if not installed);
- Software training (if required);
- If necessary, license fees to install multimedia applications;
- Production equipment (if required and not installed);
- Audio and video digitisation (in person-hours, or studio fees);
- Commission original art-work and video material;
- Purchase of copyright material, if required;
- Studio services;
- Design person-hours;
- Authoring person-hours;
- Programming person-hours;
- Production person-hours;
- Emulation and Testing;
- If necessary, manufacturing costs (disc replication).

4.7 Schedule

The compilation of a design, development and production schedule is essential for the efficient use of studio time, or for providing a completion date. As with costing, estimation may play a role, the accuracy of which will increase with greater experience. A reasonable starting point for accurate scheduling is a design network (See Fig. 4.4), within which the frequency of targets or milestones depends upon fineness of granularity. A low-level approach will yield a more accurate basis upon which to build a precise schedule, where each stage can be allocated a precise period of time.

The real function of a design network, however, is to illuminate a critical path (See Fig. 4.4), highlighting those stages whose target dates if exceeded set back the entire project. Equally, less important stages manifest themselves. For example, it might be found that certain production processes running in parallel with application development can overshoot target dates without setting back the completion date.

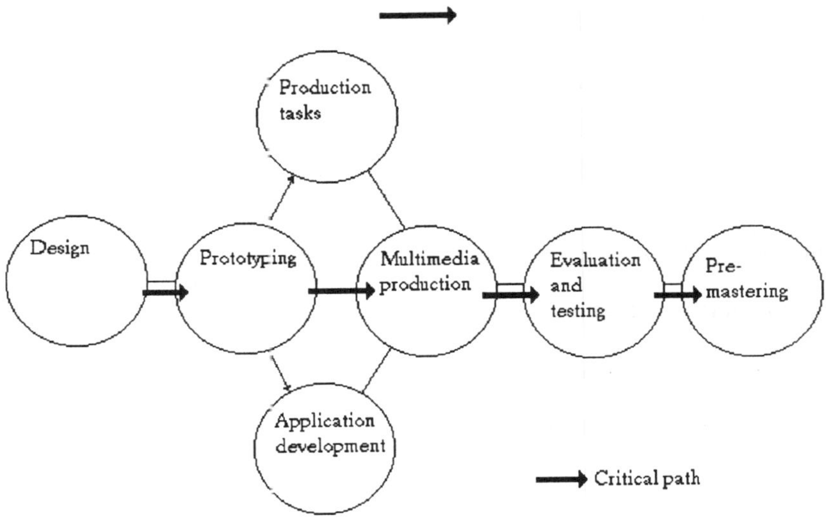

Fig 4.4: design scheduling network

4.8 Design

Though design philosophy may generally vary from one publisher/studio to the next, there is a certain amount of generic theory as to how the medium is best exploited. It is agreed, for example, that though user-interaction is a key component, its over-emphasis can result in a breakdown in user- communication.

It is also agreed that input from each component of expertise required to create a title, should exist throughout the design process, and a more significant amount of communication and consultation takes place at the outset. Done correctly, this will reveal technical constraints, unforeseen possibilities or problems, ideas and concepts.

On a technical level, design varies little from one studio to the next, with the emphasis on finding out how best to communicate information through available media types.

4.8.1 Design Team

A design team may consist of experts in all disciplines required to generate the multimedia title. A team may consist of:

- Producer/director, to enforce an appropriate degree of creative control and oversee amalgamation of media types;

- Project manager, to ensure budget and schedule are observed and adhered to;
- High-level language programmers, to design retrieval system, or to write other routines;
- Multimedia author, to implement interactive design;
- Content provider/advisor who possesses expertise in the material/information to be communicated;
- Audio visual (A-V) designer;
- Video editor (if not contracted out);
- Graphic designers/computer graphics artists, to produce original art-work;
- Sound engineers for recording etc;
- Studio technician(s);
- Various production staff.

How many of the aforementioned experts should be included, depends upon complexity of material and upon what percentage, if any, of the production process is contracted out.

4.8.2 Prototyping

Navigation, or retrieval system design, is often verified through an electronic storyboard emulation. Hypermedia authoring tools such as HyperCard provide a prototyping environment where nodes or objects can be created and linked at required levels. This permits thorough testing and fine-tuning of meaningful paths at an early stage. A CDI level 1 authoring station (See Chapter 4) can be used to generate such electronic storyboards.

Person-hours consumed during this stage of design, verification and testing, is a function of title complexity in terms of user interaction. This will be related to the number of links implanted, and to the levels at which they occur. A children's title, for instance, is likely to include a greater percentage of links at the macro level. A leisure title such as a jukebox simulation might be equally simple.

Electronic storyboards or hypermedia applications also help studios convey to clients, publishers or even investors, what can reasonably be expected from the final product in terms of functionality.

4.8.3 Multimedia Elements

The balance of multimedia elements is determined by content, volume of multimedia material, budget, the authoring station used, and delivery systems targeted.

In terms of content, common-sense is as good a guide as any to keeping each element in proportion. For example, a jukebox will require the sacrifice of a great deal of disc data capacity for the benefit of high quality stereo sound.

The finite data storage capacity of both CD-ROM and CDI discs has to be observed. This is not a matter of calculating the precise storage needs of each individual element, but can be an in-built feature of authoring software. This capability was once reasonably termed a 'constraint analyser'. Evidently, some design decisions can be made independently of content and budget.

Exact data capacity of a CD-ROM or CDI disc is function of its play time (See Chapter 2); though discs up to 79 minutes long are sometimes used, the original CD-DA format specifies 60 minutes. Queries regarding how much data can be stored should be referred either to a replication company or, perhaps, to the vendors of the multimedia authoring station/software used.

In technical terms, overall budget can influence the balance of elements and their relative quality levels. Motion video, for instance, might prove too expensive. Such a low budget which imposes constraints on creative flair can lead to imbalance where perhaps still images take precedence over motion video.

Authoring station and delivery system variants targeted, naturally play a fundamental role in determining which elements can be integrated, as well as their respective quality levels. Full-screen, full-motion video might not be an option because of limitations in delivery systems and/or authoring station, the specification of either of which might be influenced by budget. Equally, small text or detailed illustrations might be inappropriate where delivery is intended via a conventional television receiver.

4.8.4 Multimedia Development

Design, multimedia production, application development and production (See Fig. 4.5) can be considered to be the collective process necessary to formulate a multimedia title. And for distribution purposes, disc pressing constitutes a final stage.

Multimedia production can be considered as the creation and gathering of all necessary elements in appropriate form. It does not represent a new and unique set of processes, but those common to electronic publishing and A-V production.

Application development is where the all-important user-interaction is installed. Content and authoring software used also play a role, governing at which level programming occurs. Some authoring tools might require no high-level programming, generating application code automatically. More sophisticated applications often require programming using either an indigenous authoring language or general purpose high-level language such as C.

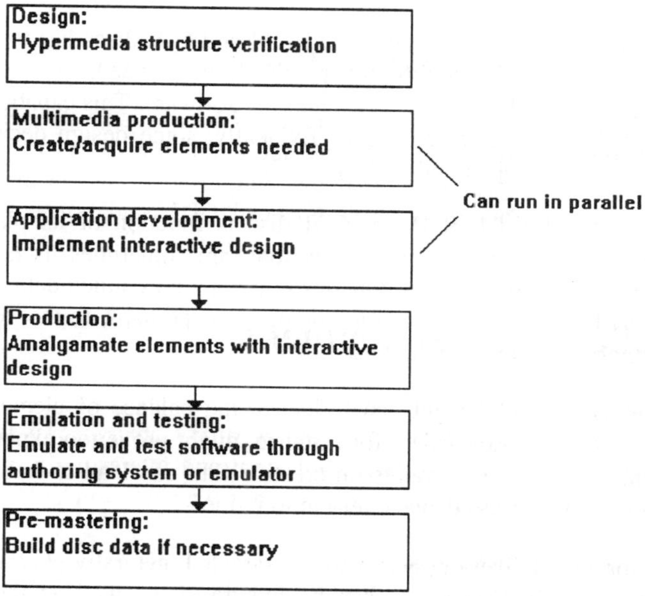

Fig 4.5

Production marries the application with all materials required, and also involves emulation and testing.

4.9 Multimedia Production

Multimedia production embodies the implementation of all tasks necessary to attain (in appropriate format) audio and visual materials required. The A-V studio environment is naturally conducive to this, where audio and visual processes are confined to separate studio areas. The following components are typical of the production process:

- Create (or acquire) and digitise still and moving images;
- Create (or acquire) and digitise text;

- Create (or acquire) audio material;
- Edit and re-touch images;
- Edit video as required;
- Edit sound sequences as required;
- Mix audio down as required;
- Convert digitised material into required file formats.

The various human resources and facilities required are available through studios and replication companies world-wide, and it is quite common for such services to be called upon, not only for production duties but also for technical advice. CDI developers can benefit from the OCDIS (Official CDI Studios) network, each of which is supported by a local Philips IMS support centre.

4.10 Application Development

Application development is perhaps the most critical stage, as it is here that the retrieval system (proven through electronic storyboard or otherwise) is finally created or adapted. A highly effective creative component and interesting mix of elements, will be subdued if the product of this stage is in any way sub-standard.

The point at which application development takes place, relative to multimedia production, is dependent upon the design network (See Fig. 4.4) or indeed the deadlines of a number of productions a studio may have in progress.

In certain circumstances the same retrieval system can be installed in different applications; jukeboxes, for example, where all that changes are, the sound tracks and other related materials. It is also possible to call upon commonly used library routines. These may have been distributed with the authoring tool itself, or they might be in-house products from previous applications.

Applications developers are normally high-level programmers, but there is considerable scope for non-programmers, particularly with simpler applications and appropriate authoring systems/tools.

The level of programming skills currently required will probably diminish in future for all but the most complex applications. This will be brought about by the emergence of more obliging authoring tools.

4.10.1 Technical Constraints

Understandably technical constraints of CD-ROM (See Chapter 2) or CDI discs, with respect to data transfer rates, access times and data capacities, can impose creative control by default. These restrictions invariably tie in with other more complex issues such as permissible quality levels of required elements. Interaction between designers and developers (and production staff) is therefore essential, providing a means of finding out what is technically possible while imparting project objectives.

The extent of such collaboration depends upon the particular multimedia authoring environment in question. For instance, storing elements in a database during multimedia production can manifest the boundaries imposed by maximum (disc) data storage capacity. It is then possible to obtain optimum quality levels permissible with little or no consultation.

4.11 Production

Marrying all elements with a retrieval system or application program is a satisfying and memorable stage in the development process. It is here that a title becomes operable and can be tested.

Easily remedied bugs of various kinds warrant a return to the application development stage for fine-tuning. More serious problems such as inappropriate paths, indicates inadequate testing at the storyboard (design) stage, and can necessitate significant modification.

Testing (in the form of a CD-simulation) requires the building of a precise disc image, which reflects the actual data content of a required CD-ROM or CDI disc. For simpler applications, testing can often be carried out from within the authoring environment.

Using compilation techniques, where machine executable object code is generated just once, the identification and subsequent correction of bugs requires a new disc image to be built. This disadvantage is accentuated by the fact that testing is an iterative process, resulting in the repetition of the often time-consuming process of disc building. Compilation speeds are therefore significant, and are naturally aided by the adoption of authoring stations which exhibit relatively high processing speeds (such as a Sun SPARC station, for example).

Interpretive techniques, where machine-executable code is generated each time the application is run, mean that results of modifications, however large or small, can be evaluated immediately. For the benefit of testing, it is therefore desirable that we see a growing number of tools incorporating this technique.

For 'CD' multimedia, the final outcome of production is disc data stored on an appropriate medium, and in a format from which a replication company can manufacture an appropriate CD-ROM or CDI disc. In the case of CDI, disc building tools will always produce the appropriate data format for submission to a CDI disc manufacturing facility. (Disc building is otherwise known as pre-mastering.)

4.12 Disc Replication

With disc data built and stored, a replication company can be employed to create a master disc and so produce a specified quantity of discs. However, where under 100 discs are required, the possibility of using CD-R replication might be considered (See Chapter 2) using such drives as the Kodak PCD Writer 200.

If uncertain about data format and submission medium requirements, advice should be sought from the replication company.

Generally, the following media are acceptable:

- Hard disk (check with company);
- Floppy disk;
- WORM disc;
- DAT, tape streamer.

Where data is in appropriate CDI or CD-ROM format, the mastering and manufacturing process (See Fig 6.4) can begin without further data manipulation. Mastering involves the physical creation of a glass disc mirroring exactly the CDI or CD-ROM disc to be produced.

In clean room conditions, an electroforming process ensures the glass master is transcribed onto metal stampers, the output from which is tested electronically as well as mechanically.

By injection moulding, clear polycarbonate pressings are produced, to which a metallic disc (holding encoded data) is bonded. Finally, the assembly is coated with a protective lacquer. At advanced manufacturing facilities, the complete manufacturing and quality control process is highly automated, where the highest level of personnel interaction will be through the operation of semi-automatic systems and quality control. Quality control normally consists of data verification, manual or automatic inspection, and microscope analysis of pit geometry (for quality analysis).

5

Hypermedia and Hypertext

"It seemed so clear to me right from the very beginning that writing should not be sequential... the problems we all have in writing sequential prose derives from the fact that we are trying to make it all lie down in one long string... if we could only break it up into different chunks that readers could choose..." – Ted Nelson

Hypermedia provides a new and previously unequalled paradigm for communicating information. For many, it will alter the popular perception of how computers and technology are used. Commercial hypermedia programs such as HyperCard and ToolBook are employed by a growing number of people. HyperCard now forms part of mainstream computing for Macintosh users. Programs or 'stacks' which run in the HyperCard environment are used for retrieval systems, CBT courseware, presentations as well as for other more specialised applications.

5.1 Terminology

Most commercial hypermedia CD titles are devoid of any reference to the terminology which has emerged from several pioneering projects. As such, the language associated with hypermedia is disappearing slightly as it makes the transition from theory to becoming a commercially available 'product'. Hypermedia packages for desktop computers complicate matters further, as there is no universal terminology. However, the following is a list of the more generic terms:

Browse - describes the process of following a path, passing to and from nodes or objects in hypermedia material, and is a micro-level activity;

Button - an active area on screen, usually iconic representation of option, feature or application, and responsive to user-interaction;

Help system - on-line help information outlining hypermedia system usage, and is usually context sensitive;

Hyperdocument - often used to describe documents, or segments of documents within hypermedia applications;

Navigation - following a path through information at the macro level, giving the user a high-level experience of the structure;

Node - micro-features of documents and images, often called chunks;

User - person interacting with hypermedia system who should not be referred to as reader;

Path - course through linked information followed by user.

The line that divides navigating from browsing is made clearer by considering the difference between the walker and the motorist. The motorist gains a high level view of travel, and is 'navigating'. The walker's experience of a journey is infinitely more detailed, hence the walker is 'browsing'.

5.2 Home Hypermedia

In the home, hypermedia can exist in many different forms ranging from HyperCard stacks on the Macintosh, to CD-ROM/XA/CDI titles covering various topics. Most will experience it through the latter where the basic mechanics of hypermedia are applied as a means of imparting information efficiently. For example, an atlas where the user is able to move through various levels of maps in order to home in on geographic locations (See Fig. 5.1).

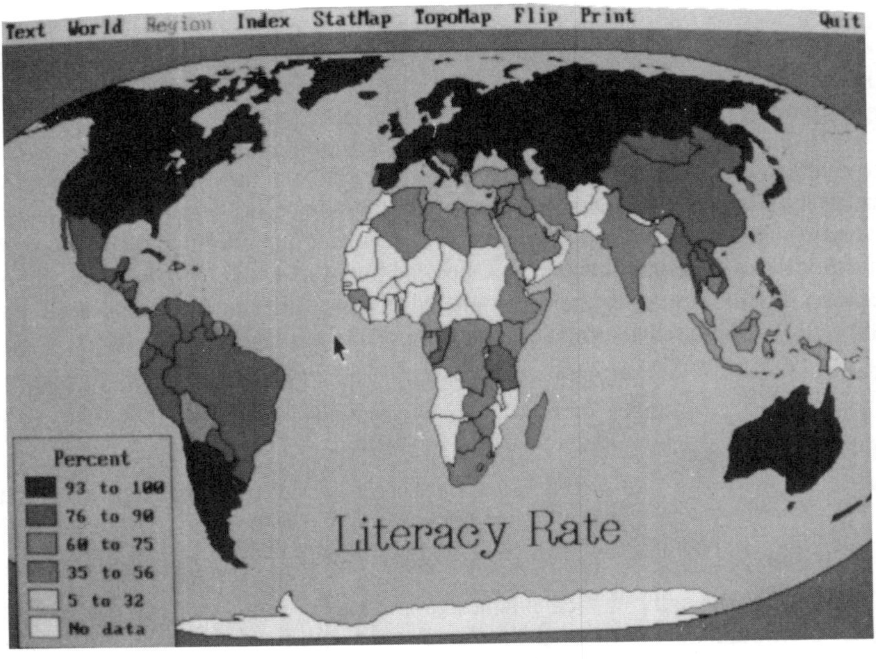

Fig 5.1 Hypermedia atlas

Similarly applied, hypermedia concepts exist, in various forms, in numerous commercially available educational titles, and in reference works of many different kinds.

Through games with realistic sound effects and video images, hypermedia also reveals a significant leisure market. Rightly or wrongly, title bases such as these will sell both consumer multimedia systems as well as those based upon desktop computers. Confined to stand-alone CD-based multimedia systems in the home, hypermedia is a far cry from Nelson's vision of a globally accessible database of published information. The realisation of a unifying information base, accessible to people throughout the world, is without doubt the ultimate aim, and we should not lose sight of this, nor let the consumer systems of today shape our views of hypermedia and multimedia too much.

5.3 Education

For literally hundreds of years, the staple tools of education have remained unchanged. Conventional text books, exercise books and blackboards remain the mandatory features for teaching and learning.

Since the early eighties, however, efforts have been made globally to bring technology into education at an extraordinary pace, with very few classrooms in the developed world now devoid of any kind of computer.

Observing the development of computers in general over the past decade, it is not difficult to imagine the realisation of the much-repeated prophecy that, for better or for worse, technology will one day replace teachers and lecturers. Such a vision becomes more feasible when hypermedia and true multimedia enter into the debate.

In the near future, however, it cannot be stressed more strongly that technology will remain an educational 'tool'. It is clear for now that CD-ROM (and CD-) based multimedia systems in schools will provide the sort of benefits which will make technology more of a necessity and less of an option. Considering the power of both CD-ROM/CDI and hypermedia, computers thus far, have for the better part been ineffective. It could be argued that a great deal of money has been wasted on behalf of the early microcomputers in education.

Hypermedia, however, will be different for a number of reasons including:

- CD-based systems and CDI players provide access to large quantities of information, composed of mixed media types, from a single access point;
- Video, a universally understandable feature of modernity, is particularly engaging for both pupils and students, thus hypermedia can form part of the accepted and understood 'language' of communication;

- Powers of association of hypermedia help pupils and students gain a thorough understanding of material;
- Developments in micro graphics and related peripherals mean that more sophisticated computer images are now possible;
- Development of hypermedia courseware helps teachers and lecturers reinforce their own knowledge.

At present, there are a number of environments in which hypermedia is supported in schools. Conventional computers provide a platform for hypermedia programs such as HyperCard and ToolBook. CD-ROM based computers, such as MPCs permit the delivery of hypermedia CD-ROM titles. Multimedia players such as CDI and CDTV also permit the delivery of hypermedia titles. It is likely that CD-ROM XA and DVI will also find their way into education in due course.

The large CBT market brings with it a number of purpose designed authoring systems such as Authorware Professional, TenCORE, LinkWay and Quest. Each of these provide environments for the development of courseware of varying complexity. For example, sophisticated CBT courseware created using Quest may comprise still and motion videodisc images, as well as audio.

5.4 Origins

"...that unifying world... it will be a storage mechanism and indexing structure... anyone can add documents to the ever-growing pool... The suppository needs to be a place we can all reach electronically through the telephone, perhaps through laser beam and satellite, through various electronic means so that through our computer screens we can bring the material we want as fast as we need it. And this has to be available to everyone everywhere." – Ted Nelson on the ultimate aims of Project Xanadu

The hypermedia concept was put forward in the forties by the visionary Vannevar Bush, Science Adviser to President Roosevelt and administrator of the wartime Manhattan Project. He believed that all published information should be made available through access points, and clearly set out the advantages of association through links. Calling the system Memex, and describing it as, "a sort of private file and library", he thought that some kind of workstation would be used with user-interaction accommodated through mechanical levers.

If there were errors in his vision, it was a total underestimation of the sheer quantity of information that would be published in future, and an overestimation of the technology of the day, i.e. microfilm, facsimile and telegraph. Even with current technology, such a system would require a massive effort on the part of publishers, information providers of all kinds, and probably government(s).

It was Bush's misfortune to live in the era of 'valves'. The solid state transistor had yet to be invented, and it was some thirty years before the first reasonably sophisticated microprocessor was made commercially available. As such, Memex remained in the minds of a select few. In more recent times, hypermedia can be associated with Ted Nelson who, it is understood, coined the term hypertext in the sixties. He devised the concept in the fall of 1960. To many, hypertext was a re-emergence of Bush's concept and Nelson himself acknowledges that he may well have read the original article on Memex Bush wrote for popular consumption in *Atlantic Monthly.*

The sixties proved a more conducive atmosphere as mainframe and minicomputers arrived. Few university campuses and research establishments were without access to these. Douglas Engelbart pioneered a system at Stanford which was to yield new terms, techniques and hardware. He developed the 'windows' environment, and used dedicated function keys to invoke a context-sensitive help system. He also introduced word processing, outline processing and user-communication through a mouse. Engelbart is accredited with the development of the experimental On-line System (NLS). The Augment System is also regarded to be his and is still in use in the aerospace industry (at McDonnell-Douglas). With its multi-user capability, ability to open multiple windows, and mouse, NLS was a milestone in the development of the modern computer.

Randall Trigg is regarded as another influential figure in shaping modern hypermedia. Most commercially available hypermedia systems take much from his Textnet thesis. This puts forward the popular chunk-based model for hypertext, where the user is tied to the author's implanted link structures which relate micro-features of the hypermedia system. Trigg also offers the idea of typed links that are user-defined. Link names are also included, describing the relationship between nodes. The transition, from character displays and character graphics to bitmap graphics, introduced images into the hypertext equation, thus giving hypermedia.

The seventies saw the development of the hypertext system ZOG at Carnegie-Mellon University. Among other applications it was used for conferencing and CBT. ZOG is best known for its role on the USS *Carl Vinson* where it is used as a ship-wide information and management system. Incorporating graphics, the Knowledge Management System (KMS) is the commercial face of ZOG. Both ZOG and KMS adopt the frame-based approach, where whole documents or frames are linked. Each frame is made up of text objects. Many of today's commercial implementations adopt this technique. The introduction of HyperCard in 1987 by Apple Computer was the most notable milestone in its commercial evolution.

With many millions of microcomputers now installed in homes world-wide, and with more advanced communications, the 'Memex' notion becomes infinitely more feasible. It is within this new environment that Nelson continues to develop his brain-child, Xanadu, a globally accessible database of literature and other published information. An expandable pool of published material, it is the ultimate electronic book, and is intended to monitor user activity and so produce royalty statements and demands. However, this is Project Xanadu rather the current commercial implementations called 'Xanadu'. A 'Xanadu' prototype front-end is now available for workstations, as is a prototype storage engine. Xanadu Operating Company also provide the Xanadu document server for single users and LANs, as well as a multi-server storage and delivery program. The company will soon offer a much-talked-about automatic royalty service. Nelson envisages Xanadu as becoming a global network of public access terminal stations, used in much the same way as public libraries. Public-access open hypertext publishing can then become reality.

5.5 Links

At a superficial level, there is a degree of overlap between the hypermedia and relational database models. Both share the idea of association through links. Unlike databases, however, hypermedia links can provide low-level paths which do not exist solely for the convenience of data storage. For example, they can possess directionality.

Database links such as one-to-one, one-to-many, many-to-one, and many-to-many are shared by hypertext and hypermedia. However, there are technical variations in how these are perceived by software producers and designers. In the case of a multi-table form within a relational database, such links can refer to how 'master' tables and 'detail' tables are associated (See Fig. 5.2) as follows:

One-to-one - each master record is linked to only one detail record at any given time;

One-to-many - each master record is linked to a group of detail records;

Many-to-one - a number of master records may be linked to a single detail record;

Many-to-many - each master record is one of a group which can be matched to one of a group of detail records.

At a structural level, hypermedia is quite different from the relational database model, and hypermedia users have quite different objectives in mind.

Placed in the context of hypermedia, links of association are taken to more extreme limits. Nodes, representing text or images, are linked to provide a potentially infinite number of meaningful paths. For example, a single node representing a linear structure, such as an article, might be linked to numerous other articles and images.

Links can naturally exist at a number of levels, either to link complete documents (macro features), or to reference words or phrases (micro-features) within documents.

The former approach is widespread. It is this face of hypermedia which is seen on virtually all commercially available implementations.

Nelson stipulates a preference for the implantation of links at the micro-level, where single words, phrases or image fragments can be linked. Project Xanadu is intended to permit the existence of links at all levels. In Nelson parlance the three categories of link are:

Point-to-point;

Point-to-span;

Span-to-span.

Points can be micro features such as words, phrases, sentences or image fragments. A span is a higher level node such as a block of text, document or image.

The byte level, or low-level, approach used in Xanadu, facilitates the extraction of data at all levels from stored documents. Resultant 'fragment showers' can be used to produce virtual documents. This cannot be achieved through a rigid high-level frame-based system.

Virtual documents are similar to the concept of compound documents which are now entering into mainstream computing.

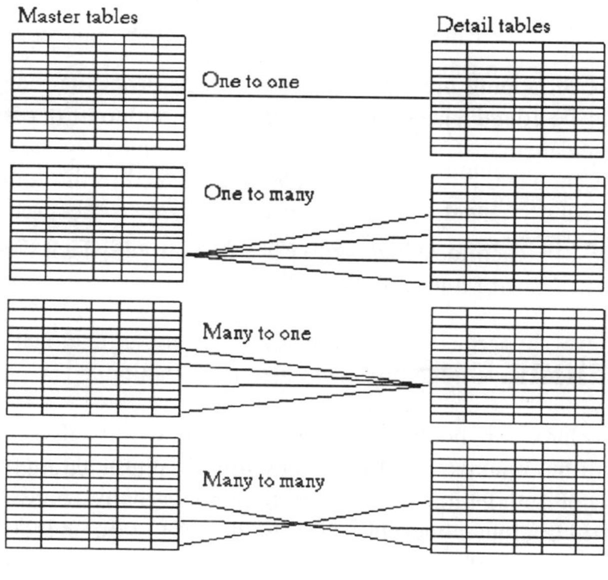

Fig 5.2

5.5.1 Structure

The structure of a hypermedia application determines its overall effectiveness. Hierarchical or tree structures are well known and are normally represented using unidirectional links. Strict hierarchy (See Fig 5.3) demands that objects are only accessible through a parent. Compromised hierarchy, however, is less formal, permitting links to bypass children objects.

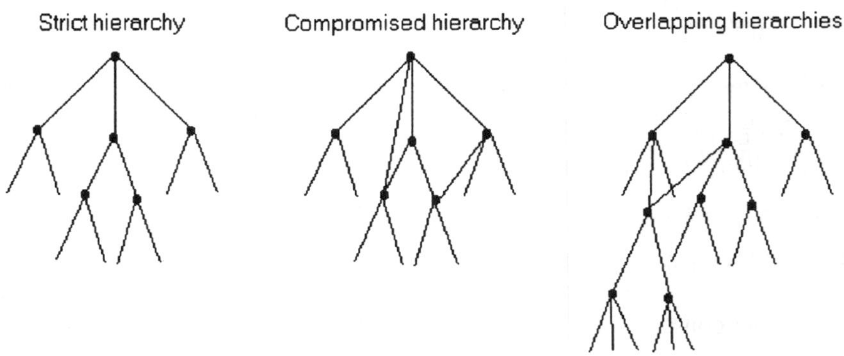

Fig 5.3

A classic problem with strict hierarchical hypermedia is the rigidity of paths; they become almost linear. Portions of information attained can deviate by varying amounts from what the user wishes to know or understand.

Comprised and overlapping hierarchies also have their problems. For example, if the same object can be found via dissimilar paths, then the context of user interaction cannot always be satisfied. Take, for example, the user pursuing the subject of Wales and the Welsh Language. A document or chunk dedicated to the formation of S4C – the Welsh television channel – might only be relevant to the user studying media within the country of Wales. This phenomenon was once referred to as the Chunking Problem.

5.6 Publishing

Hypermedia and hypertext could mark the beginning of a renaissance in publishing, radically altering the manner in which information is presented and used. Perhaps a growing portion of authors and writers, having only recently become accustomed to submitting text in computer readable form (and perhaps using DTP), will see their work methods undergo further and more fundamental change. It is unlikely, however, that this will occur with anything like the speed of the introduction of the word processor.

It can be argued that writing a book, using a hypertext or hypermedia authoring tool, provides a better medium for most authors, and would be particularly helpful in generating the kinds of rigourous structures prevalent in technical and educational texts. For the immediate future, the distribution of such books is likely to take place through 'CD' and later through a more compact medium. Its commercial success is, therefore, tied in with the growth rate of the relevant user base(s). In addition, the introduction of commercially successful portable electronic books may also represent an important factor.

The Australian Smart Book, a portable system that uses ROM packs is capable of storing up to 45 Mbytes of compressed text. Currently, it can be said that the advantages of using ROM are:

- Shorter access times;
- Potentially higher data transfer rates;
- Low power consumption;
- Reduced risk of electromechanical failure;
- More compact construction than the standard 12cm-diameter CD-ROM.

Whichever technology is adopted, portable books must not only support hypertext and in the longer term hypermedia, but also behave in a similar way to conventional books/documents. For example, a means of annotation must be supported, together with the ability to restart a system to find a previous session of user-interaction exactly 'as you left it' (AYLI – 'aily'). In addition, markers should remain active on storage media themselves, thus giving a perfect emulation of a bookmark. Finally, any storage media used must be extremely compact and easily removed and inserted. Ideally, the storage medium should be capable of storing hundreds, and perhaps thousands, of publications. The user would be able to read publications purchased by unlocking them.

A fundamental problem with the current standard CD variants, adopted as a publishing medium for hypertext, hypermedia or otherwise, is the user-intensive operation of changing disks. This is complicated further by the need to use caddies on many rather primitive drives and players. The E-library concept, for example, might prove a great disappointment for this reason.

However, just like the combustion engine has proved enduring, current standard CD technology may also remain longer than we would like.

Hypertext and hypermedia become infinitely more effective when moving away from the stand-alone or local network system concept, toward the notion of a common access world depository of published information. Just how far such a system could be taken is, of course, infinite. For example, everything from daily news to modern literature could be made available through terminals in homes, offices, schools, colleges and universities.

5.7 Hypermedia Flaws

It can be argued that current commercial hypermedia implementations are far from perfect. Understandably, we tend to see the most primitive facets of hypermedia theory put into practice.

Even the full-blown hypermedia concept as it stands is not flawless, and subjected to critical, but not overly critical, examination, certain limitations, weaknesses and questions occur. For example, taken to extreme limits, would an initiative such as Project Xanadu simply offer too much by way of choice, leaving average users knowing a little about a great many topics and a great deal about nothing?

Like Bush before him, Nelson wholly believes in the potential of hypermedia to augment man's intellect. However, this belief is based on an optimistic view of the hypermedia user and public in general. For example, it is a fact that quality television programmes, films and newspapers rarely achieve the larger audiences. Such commercial pressure may well come to bear upon hypermedia. Though, what is currently regarded as commercially appealing, is by no means a constant.

5.7.1 'Over Efficiency'

What is being proposed through hypermedia is another step toward harnessing technology to achieve yet greater efficiency. Impatience, and an ever-decreasing concentration span, represent two off-shoots of this trend. For example, remote control television seems to cajole viewers to see a small percentage of a number of programmes and all of nothing. Similarly the computer user will complain about the slow speed of a DTP program or word processor that actually allows him/her to work very fast when compared to techniques used less than ten years ago.

New generations that have not experienced part of, or all of, the full cycle of development are particularly prone to complaint, e.g. word processor operators who have never had to use a typewriter.

Hypermedia is yet another concept which may have similar effects. The idea of individuals interacting with hypermedia/hypertext every day, and having never read what we 'now' perceive as a complete book from start to finish, concerns many, as do the effects of users 'document-hopping' from one book to another. Could this lead to fewer individuals unable to read and 'enjoy' anything resembling a continuous, linear stream of text?

5.7.2 The Hypermedia Platform

"Here we have a medium that incorporates every other medium that ever came before it – ranging all the way from graphics, as in cave paintings, to text, to television, to auditory communication like the telephone – and create integrated worlds in which all these things are together for the first time. This form incorporates everything that can be incorporated. It incorporates experience itself."

"The enthusiasm over VR is another example of what Paul Sapho calls macro-myopia, which is the willingness of society to overestimate the short-term effects of technological breakthrough and underestimate its long-term effects. Let's take, for example, computers. Some people regarded them as toys, or another one of these things from California, until one day that they woke up and found out that computers were everywhere, that they were a functional part of their lives as much as toasters."

– John Barlow on virtual reality

Not that the author is given to peeping through keyholes, but for many applications, the computer monitor is rather like a small keyhole through which you are trying to view the contents of a room. This 'tunnel vision' is particularly noticeable when using computers to access vast databases of information; it can be difficult to gain an overall picture of how the information is linked.

The computer monitor is clumsy when performing any kind of operation that requires more than one document on screen simultaneously. The windows concept helps, but if there is not enough room for two windows or documents on screen at the same time, then they cannot appear together.

Though hypermedia/hypertext helps overcome this problem to a reasonable degree, conventional computer monitors and computers remain prohibitive; the screen size sets frustrating limitations and user-interaction is too awkward. It seems that, if we are serious about hypermedia, the computer monitor must not reside on the desktop but it must *be* the desktop or an appropriately large 'surface'. It must be responsive to touch (or perhaps speech) and it must be possible to move and place material from one place (or application) to the next. The QWERTY keyboard (if required) can be physical, or preferably an emulation or metaphor which can be moved from one location to the next.

The ultimate solution is virtual reality (VR) within which, perhaps, ergonomic environments conducive to many different requirements could be simulated. Wearing a Head Mount Display (HMD) (or EyePhone™) fitted with LCDs (which provide an appropriately wide angle of vision) and headphones, the user is presented with a 3-D virtual environment. Today this environment is generated using relatively crude computer graphics.

Through user interaction made recognisable by wearing Data Gloves™ or even complete 'suits' fitted with optic sensors, the possibilities of opening windows (screen areas), or even working at a virtual keyboard, arise. Current rate of advancement of VR technology points to a maturity which is a great deal closer than many individuals, ignorant or otherwise, might care to, or even like to, admit.

5.8 Case Study – CBT Courseware Development

Throughout the text, authoring systems/tools and authoring stations have been referred to on numerous occasions. In Chapter 4 the multimedia authoring process was discussed in the perspective of CD, with attention paid to commercial considerations.

Here we look at just what is involved in creating some Computer-based Training (CBT) courseware. This will manifest what can be achieved through a typical authoring system/tool.

You will probably be surprised by the types of problems which become apparent. It is the unexpected which frequently causes developers to go off on tangents, away from the neat theoretical process outlined in the previous chapter.

This design case study begins with a brief to develop a software training package. The program in question is a custom Relational Database Management System (RDBMS). As the CBT courseware to be developed is for in-house consumption, many of the marketing aspects of a commercial title, are neglected.

The design brief is as follows:

To produce CBT courseware suitable for training new employees how to use an in-house RDBMS. The courseware is to be made available simultaneously on 14 different sites, the closest pair of which are 64 miles apart.

There must be a high degree of user-interaction, and students' performance is to be monitored. Scores attained by students must also be made available in report and graph form to training managers.

The material itself must consist of program simulations and of a number of multiple choice questions which pertain to everyday operation of the database.

Everyday database usage includes searching for files, sending letters, printing reports, querying tables and producing graphs.

As it is necessary to tender for the contract, we naturally begin by costing the proposed project.

5.8.1 Costing

It is apparent from the brief that motion video is not required. This will reduce the cost of delivery, permitting the installation of systems devoid of video cards.

Also evident is the fact that audio will not be required, and this too will lead to savings.

Recalling from Chapter 4 the components which must be considered, only the following apply in this case:

- Multimedia delivery systems;
- Authoring system/tool;
- Licence fees to install multimedia applications;
- Commission original art-work;
- Design person-hours;
- Authoring person-hours;
- Production person-hours;
- Emulation and Testing.

The specification of the delivery systems required is a function of which authoring system is used. In this case any IBM PC AT or compatible with EGA/VGA graphics can be used. For improved performance, 386 systems with colour VGA graphics will be used. They will also require a 40 Mbyte hard disk to support the estimated size of the final training application.

The fact that the application must monitor the performance of each student dictates the type of authoring system that can be used. *Quest* from Allen Communication is one such system which permits the integration of such features into applications, and is chosen here. Quest was also chosen for its ability to develop applications which can be run on any PC. So if the budget were to prove inadequate due to unforeseen circumstances, there would be capacity to economise by opting for lower specification PCs.

Licence fees to install applications vary from one company to the next. For example, the following licence arrangements are frequently offered:

- Install a specified number of applications per copy of authoring system;
- Pay fixed fee for the installation of single application;
- Purchase a limited licence which permits installation of specified number of applications;
- Purchase unlimited licence that enables the installation of a limitless number of applications.

In this case, the vendors offered all of the above options, and the last of these proved the most economical.

Though art-work was required for only the opening screen, the services of an artist were purchased. The same artist/graphic designer also assisted in choosing appropriate fonts, colours and screen layouts.

Most of the required images were to be captured in appropriate image files and then loaded into the authoring system. Program simulations were also to be constructed in the same way. Person-hours consumed through design, authoring, emulation and testing were estimated. It was not clear at the outset whether or not programming would be necessary.

5.8.2 Design network

Having estimated the cost of the entire development process, and submitted a tender, we have succeeded in winning the contract. With the prospect of a return for the unpaid work implemented thus far, we are now in a position to begin the design and development.

Now we can embark on the creation of a design network, so as to isolate a critical path and to ensure that the various phases of development are coordinated correctly. Network granularity need not be so fine so as to highlight micro-phases, such as the creation of a single screen layout, but should exist at a level which ensures that all the major tasks are implemented in the correct order (See Fig. 5.5).

5.8.3 Authoring System

On numerous occasions throughout the text, the term authoring system has been used and references have been made to the various features they may offer. We now have an opportunity to see just what can be done with typical authoring system such as Quest. This package is aimed expressly at the development of CBT courseware and has the ability to control a videodisc player. It is comparable to Authorware Professional and TenCORE, though it is great deal less expensive than the former. In addition Authorware Professional has evolved into a more general-purpose authoring system.

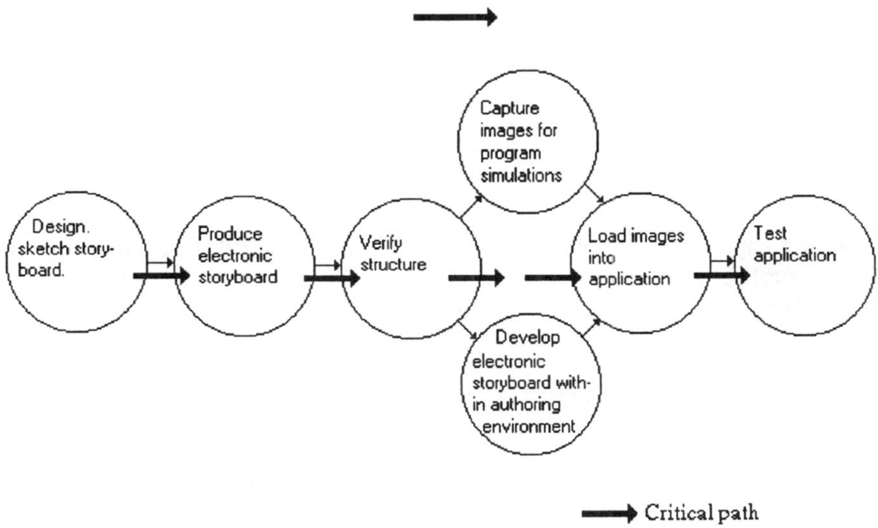

Fig 5.5

Quest is a frame-based system, and though it has its own language QAL (Quest Authoring Language), applications can be created in a menu driven environment.

Lessons are constructed from a number of frames each of which contain a number of objects. Objects include text, images and branches. You can edit any frame at random. However, objects cannot be edited, instead they have to be erased and then re-established in the required form.

Quest is particularly flexible in terms of monitoring the performance of students. Indeed it is for this reason that it was chosen.

It is also possible to create interesting animations. Cycle animations, where a number of images are presented in turn, can be used for micons, though in reality they are rarely used for this purpose. Path animations, where an image is simply moved from one point to another, are easily created: you simply define the path using the arrow keys. However, the version used for this production was unable to load animations from other programs.

5.8.4 Design

Before actually designing the courseware, an understanding of the particular RDBMS being used had to be grasped. A combination of operating the database and information gathering yielded this.

At this early and most important development stage, input from the training manager was essential. Advice was needed on the scoring of questions and tasks within the courseware, and on which areas of operation should be emphasised. With an understanding of what were perceived as important topics and how questions should be scored, the application's structure could be addressed.

Rather than immediately delving into a suitable program (such as HyperCard) to do this, pen and paper were initially used, although only as a prelude to generating an electronic storyboard. It also provided a forum for suggestions and input from various members of the design team, as well as from client representatives.

5.8.5 Electronic Storyboard

It was discovered that Quest possessed a flowchart feature which presented instant overviews of lessons. To benefit from this, it was decided that Quest should be used to generate a storyboard, though this would not contain any images or program simulations but only concise descriptions.

Now we arrive at the first technical hitch. Though the developers involved had much experience of using multimedia authoring systems, nobody had Quest experience. Software training and subsequent telephone support became the order of the day. Though this was by no means unanticipated, it represented a minor set-back which we could have done without.

However, that we could implement storyboards with Quest meant that this prototyping phase would overlap into application development thus optimising design and development time.

5.8.6 Multimedia Production

We now arrive at the fork in the design network, where we see both multimedia production and application development processes running in parallel. With all the program images and simulations decided, multimedia production could begin. Production was simple in this case, merely comprising the acquisition of screen images from the RDBMS so as they could be imported into Quest.

It is here that a second technical hitch arose. It was discovered that the particular version of Quest being used would load .IMG images only. Rather than using the

Quest Capture Image program, a member of the team spent many hours on site capturing images in the form of .IMG files using a tried and tested 'capture' program. It was not until the production stage that it was realised that the Quest .IMG file format was not the accepted standard and none of the acquired images could be loaded.

Using the Capture Image program to acquire all the images once again resulted in the loss of a complete morning. We were on the critical path and the whole project was now being set back, leaving team members inactive and restless.

This most embarrassing of incidents did not end there. Rather than loading a sample image into quest to ensure that the images were 100% compatible, as should have been done in the first place, it was left to the 'culprit' to work through every break and acquire all images once again.

Yet again they proved incompatible. The problem this time hinged on the fact the images had been captured in the wrong graphics mode. For some reason a dusty CGA system had been used, and we were working in VGA. This particular version of Quest had no facility for converting images to and from different graphics standards.

A further afternoon had been wasted. We all went off to the site the next morning and managed to capture all images in under two hours. For obvious reasons we were furtive enough to ensure the client learned nothing of our incompetence. This whole episode resulted in the loss of ten hours. Until this point we had maintained a position of being two full days ahead of schedule. Though, it should be said that the version of Quest we were using was particularly inflexible in that it lacked openness in regard to accepting different image file formats.

The text objects required for the application could not be prepared at any time other than during application development itself.

A computer artist was commissioned to produce an opening splash screen. This was to show the client company logo and so forth, in an effort to make the application both professional in appearance and aesthetically pleasing.

The actual screen was produced using Corel Draw and was captured using the Quest Capture Image program.

5.8.7 Application Development

Storyboard and application development formed a continuum, representing the same rather lengthy process.

With branches already implanted at the storyboard stage, application development consisted largely of creating text objects, and establishing answer criteria. In the event of expected incorrect answers the student would be prompted with pertinent hints.

Several program simulations were considered best left to the production stage. This was to prove a major misjudgment in fact, as confining the creation of program simulations to application development would have revealed the incompatibility of image files at an earlier stage.

5.8.8 Production

Production proved a particularly arduous process for reasons already outlined. We also had the problem of a minor overlap between application development and production brought about by the necessity to create program simulations.

However, the marriage of images with the existing application structure was assisted by the fact that the 'lesson' could be tested 'on the fly'.

5.8.9 Testing and Training

With the application complete, and having implemented some superficial testing at the production stage, it was necessary to test the actual application proper. Loading up the application on several different stations, we all became beta-testers.

Testing yielded several missing branches and a number of awkward sentences in text objects. Their correction meant revisiting the application development stage. As is common, this proved an iterative process.

With the application complete (four days behind schedule) it was now left to teach training managers how to use the newly developed courseware.

Appendix A

Multimedia Delivery/Authoring Station Manufacturers

Commodore Business Machines Ltd (UK)
Commodore House
The Switchback
Gardner Road
Maidenhead
Berks, SL6 7XA. Tel: 0628 770088; Fax: 0628 71456

CompuAdd
Tel: 0272 254789
IBM (UK)
PO Box 117
Mountbatten House
Basing View
Basingstoke
Hampshire, RG21 1EJ. Tel: 0256 56144; Fax: 0256 479366

IBM (UK)
National Enquiry Centre
389 Chiswick High Road
London, W4 4AL. Tel: 081 747 0747

Intel Semiconductor of Canada, Ltd
190 Attwell Drive
Suite 500
Rexdale
Ontario, M9W 6H8. Tel: 416 675 2105

Intel Corporation (U.K.) Ltd
Pipers Way
Swindon
Wiltshire, SN3 1RJ. Tel: 0793 696000

Intel Corporation US
3065 Bowers Avenue
Santa Clara
CA 95051. Tel: 408 765 8080

Microvitec plc (UK)
Futures Way
Bolling Road
Bradford
West Yorkshire, BD4 7TU. Tel: 274 390011; Fax: 274 734944

NEC (UK) Ltd
NEC House
1 Victoria Road
Acton
London, W3 6UL. Tel: 081 9938111; Fax: 081 9936499

Sony Broadcast and Communication Products Company (UK)
Jays Close
Viables
Basingstoke
Hampshire, RG22 4SB.
Tel: 0256 474011; Fax: 0256 816397

Tandy GRiD
Tel: 081 897 6565

Appendix B

CD-ROM Drive Manufacturers

Hitachi Sales (UK) Ltd
Hitachi House
Station Road
Hayes
Middx, UB3 4DR.
Tel: 071 848 8787

Mitsumi
UK Distributor:
UK Flex Ltd
6 Westfield Road
Birmingham,,B27 7TL.
Tel: 021 624 7777; Fax: 021 624 4835

NEC (UK) Ltd
NEC House
1 Victoria Road
Acton
London, W3 6UL.
Tel: 081 9938111; Fax: 081 9936499

Philips IMS
Freeland House,
Station Road
Dorking
Surrey, RH4 1UL
Tel: +44 306 75777; Fax: +44 306 75779

Pioneer Laser Technology (UK)
Field Way
Greenford
Middlesex, UB6 8UZ. Tel: 081 575 8040

Sony Broadcast & Communication Products Company (UK)
Jays Close
Viables
Basingstoke
Hampshire, RG22 4SB. Tel: 0256 474011; Fax: 0256 816397

US

Denon America
222 New Road
Parsippany
NJ 077054. Tel: 201 575 7810

Digital Equipment Corporation
2 Mount Royal Avenue
Marlboro
MA 01752. Tel: 800 258 1710

Hitachi Sales Corporation of America
401 West Artesia Boulevard
Compton
CA 90220. Tel: 800 262 1502

JVC
41 Slater Drive
Elmwood Park
NJ 07404. Tel: 201 794 3900

Laser Magnetic Storage International
4425 Arrows West Drive
Colorado Springs
CO 80907. Tel: 303 593 4269

Laser Optical Technology
10 Victor Square
Suite 600
Scotts Valley
CA 95066. Tel: 408 426 7171

NEC Home Electronics
1255 Michael Drive
Wood Dale
IL 60191-1094. Tel: 312 860 9500

Panasonic
1 Panasonic Way
Secaucus
NJ 07094. Tel: 201 392 4602

Philips Player Information
Philips Consumer Electronics Co.
IMS Sales Division
One Philips Drive
Knoxville, TN 37914-1810. Tel: 615 521 4706

Reference Technology
5700 Flatiron Parkway
Boulder
CO 80301. Tel: 303 449 4157

Sanyo
51 Joseph Street
Moonachie
NJ 07074. Tel: 201 440 9300

Sony
655 River Oaks Parkway
San Jose
CA 95134. Tel: 408 432 0190

Toshiba
9740 Irvine Boulevard
Irvine
CA 92680. Tel: 714 583 3117

Appendix C

Disc Replication Facilities

UK

Nimbus Information Systems
Wyastone Leys
Monmouth
Gwent, NP5 3SR. Tel: 0600 890682

US

3M
3M Centre, Optical Recording Department, Building 223-5S-01
St. Paul, MN 55144. Tel: 612 733 1110

American Helix Technology Corporation
1857 Colonial Village Lane
Lancaster, PA 17601. Tel: 800 525 6575

Capitol Industries/EMI
3 Capitol Way
Jacksonville, IL 62650. Tel: 217 245 9631

DADC
1800 North Fruitridge Avenue
Terre Haute, IN 47804. Tel: 812 466 6821

Denon America
1380 Monticello Road
Madison, GA 30650. Tel: 404 342 3425

Denon America
222 New Road
Parsippany, NJ 07054. Tel: 201 575 7810

Discovery Systems
7001 Discovery Boulevard
Dublin, OH 43017. Tel: 614 761 2000

Disctronics Inc
4905 Mooresmill Road
Huntsville, AL 35881. Tel: 205 859 9042

Disctronics Inc
1120 Cosby Way
Anaheim, CA 92806. Tel: 714 630 6700

JVC Disc America Inc
2 JVC Road
Tuscaloosa, AL 35405. Tel: 205 556 7111

Memory Technology Inc
2800 Summit Avenue
Plano, TX 75074. Tel: 214 881 8800

Nimbus Records Inc.
P.O. Box 7305
Charlottesville, VA 22906. Tel: 804 985 1100

Philips and Du Pont Optical
1409 Foulk Road
Wilmington, DE 19803. Tel: 302 479 2500

Philips and Du Pont Optical
Kings Mountain
Highway 29
Grover, NC 28073. Tel: 800 433 3475

Sony Laser Products
1767 Sheridan Street
Richmond, IN 47374. Tel: 317 935 7574

Shape Optimedia
Route 109 & Eagle Drive
Sanford, ME 04073. Tel: 207 324 1124

Appendix D

Authoring Systems/Tools

Audio Visual Connection (AVC)
System: PC/IBM PS/2
Description: Widely used for presentations, provides audio and video capture facilities through the presence of M-Motion Video Adapter/A. Able to control video disc player.
Supplier: IBM
Tel: 081 747 0747 (UK)

Authology
System: DVI authoring system (See Chapter 5)
Description: Multimedia authoring tool embodying full-motion video and high quality audio.
Supplier: Thorn EMI
Tel: 0628 822181 (UK)

Authorware Professional
Description: Icon-based authoring environment aimed at development of courseware and educational material. Authorware Academic is black and white, and does not possess many of the more advanced features.
Supplier: Systems Interactive
Tel: 071 728 3636 (UK)

FrameMaker
System: Workstation and DEC computers
Description: Hypermedia authoring tool incorporating AI techniques. Useful for CBT and on-line document distribution.
Supplier: Frontline
Tel: 0706 351466 (UK)

HyperDoc
System: PC
Description: Hypermedia authoring program able to control videodisc player.
Supplier: HyperDoc PLC
Tel: 081 541 1877 (UK)

HyperTies
System: Available for workstation and PC
Description: Hypermedia authoring tool
Supplier: University of Maryland
Tel: 301 454 4255 (US)

KMS
System: Workstation
Description: Frame-based hypermedia authoring system (See Chapter 4).
Supplier: Scribe Systems Inc
Tel: 412 281 5959 (US)

LinkWay Live!
System: PC XT/AT, PS/2
Description: Hypertext/hypermedia authoring environment. Extremely low-cost, popular in education sector. Requires appropriate adapter cards for sound and analogue motion emanating from videodisc player.
Supplier: IBM
Tel: 081 747 0747 (UK)

Mediascript
System: DVI authoring system (See Chapter 5)
Description: Script-based multimedia authoring program.
Supplier: Thorn EMI
Tel: 0628 822181 (UK)

Multimedia Developers Toolkit (SDK)
System: PC (Windows 3.1 class)
Description: Programming environment and tools aimed at MPC software development.
Supplier: Microsoft Ltd
Tel: 0734 270000 (UK)
Fax: 0734 270002 (UK)

NoteCards
System: Workstation
Description: Hypertext authoring tool
Supplier: Artificial Intelligence Ltd
Tel: 0923 247707 (UK)

Supplier: Xerox Palo Alto Research Centre
Tel: 415 494 4000 (US)

PictureBook
System: PC
Description: Authoring environment
Supplier: Digithurst
Tel: 0763 242955 (UK)

Quest
System: Any EGA/VGA PC
Description: Authoring system aimed at the development of CBT courseware.
Supplier: Synergy Information Systems Ltd
Tel: 0243 531155 (UK)
Supplier: Allen Communication Inc
Tel: (801) 537 7800 (US)

Storyboard Live!
System: IBM PC or PS/2 with EGA or VGA graphics
Description: Authoring environment for multimedia presentations, commonly used for business presentations.
Supplier: IBM
Tel: 081 747 0747 (UK)

TenCORE
System: PC
Description: IV development environment.
Supplier: Systems Interactive
Tel: 071 278 3636 (UK)

ToolBook
System: PC running Windows
Description: Hypermedia authoring environment.
Supplier: Softsell - Produced by Asymetrix
Tel: 081 568 8866 (UK)

TopClass
System: PC
Description: IV development environment intended for video training applications.
Supplier: TopClass Technology
Tel: 0773 820011 (UK)

Video for Windows (VfW)
System: PC (Windows 3.1 class)

Description: Video capture and play-back software; permits video clips to be integrated into numerous Windows programs.
Supplier: Microsoft Ltd
Tel: 0734 270000 (UK)
Fax: 0734 270002 (UK)

Xanadu
System: Workstation
Description: Xanadu commercial implementation (See Chapter 4)
Supplier: Xanadu Operating Company
Tel: 415 856 4112 (US)
Supplier: Autodesk Inc
Tel: 415 332 2344 (US)

Appendix E

Video Recorder/Boards

ActionMedia 750 Capture Board
System: Specific to either AT or MCA bus
Description: Real-time motion video capture and compression board.
Supplier: Intel
Tel: 408 765 8080 (US)
Tel: 0793 696000 (UK)

ActionMedia 750 Delivery Board
System: Specific to either AT or MCA bus
Description: Motion video delivery device. Decompresses data laid using the ActionMedia 750 Capture Board.
Supplier: Intel
Tel: 408 765 8080 (US)
Tel: 0793 696000 (UK)

ATVista
System: PC
Description: 32-bit video capture card
Supplier: Techex
Tel: 0628 777800 (UK)

DVA-4000
System: Available for PC, PS/2 and Macintosh
Description: Full motion digital video adapter
Supplier: VideoLogic
Tel: 0923 260511 (UK)

Harlequin 1500
System: Amiga

Description: 24-bit frame buffer
Supplier: Amiga Centre Scotland
Tel: 031 5574242 (UK)

Harlequin 4000
System: Amiga 2000 or 3000
Description: dual 24-bit frame buffers each with alpha channels
Supplier: Amiga Centre Scotland
Tel: 031 5574242 (UK)

Microeye PB card
System: Available for PC and PS/2
Description: Real-time video digitiser and video adapter
Supplier: Digithurst
Tel: 0763 242955 (UK)

M-Motion Video Adapter/A
System: PS/2
Description: Video/audio capture board.
Supplier: IBM
Tel: 081 747 0747 (UK)

Smart Video Recorder
System: PC
Description: Real-time motion video capture and compression board.
Supplier: Intel
Tel: 408 765 8080 (US)
Tel: 0793 696000 (UK)

Video Blaster
System: PC AT
Description: Low cost and surprisingly flexible video card
Supplier: West Point Creative
Tel: 0743 236605 (UK)

Video Spygot
System: PC AT
Description: Low cost and surprisingly flexible video card
Supplier: West Point Creative
Tel: 0743 236605 (UK)

Appendix F

Graphics and Animation Packages

Add Impact
System: Windows 3.1 (or higher) class PC
Description: Permits the creation of animations that can be added to Windows OLE applications
Supplier: Gold Disk
Tel: 071 498 3275

Animation Works Interactive
System: Windows 3.1 (or higher) class PC
Description: Permits the creation of vector-based animations for integration into OLE applications
Supplier: Gold Disk
Tel: 071 498 3275

Autodesk Animator Pro
System: PC
Description: Sophisticated animation package that runs from DOS
Supplier: Autodesk
Tel: 0483 303322 (UK)

Autodesk 3D Studio
System: PC
Description: 3D modelling, rendering and animation package
Supplier: Autodesk
Tel: 0483 303322 (UK)

Corel Draw!
System: PC
Description: Graphics package

Supplier: Frontline
Tel: 0256 463344 (UK)
Supplier: Softsell
Tel: 081 568 8866 (UK)
Supplier: Xitan
Tel: 0703 899321 (UK)

Media Blitz
System: Windows 3.1 (or higher) class PC
Description: Permits animations to implanted in OLE applications
Supplier: Softsell - Produced by Asymetrix
Tel: 081 568 8866 (UK)

Windows 3.1
System: PC AT and PS/2
Description: Multi-tasking environment with Paintbrush accessory. Possible to capture text screens also.
Supplier: Microsoft
Tel: 0734 391123 (UK)

Appendix G

Sound Cards

Gloria
System: PC
Description: Digitiser and play-back system, suitable for Autodesk Animator.
Supplier: Jovian Logic
Tel: 0273 208103 (UK)

Microsoft Windows Sound System
System: PC/MPC
Description: 8-bit sound card specifically for Microsoft Windows
Supplier: Microsoft Ltd
Tel: 0734 270000 (UK)
Fax: 0734 270002 (UK)

Pro Audio Spectrum
System: PC/MPC
Description: 8-bit sound card, controller for Sony CD-ROM drive.
Supplier: The Graphics Resource
Tel: 0706 217744 (UK)
Supplier: MediaVision
Tel: (0101) 415 7708600 (US)
Supplier: Access Computer
Tel: (010 49) 89 420 0601 (Germany)
Supplier: Ubisoft
Tel: (010 331) 48 576552 (France)
Supplier: Modo
Tel: (010 39) 522 512828 (Italy)

Roland LAPC 1
System: PC
Description: MIDI sound card for the PC with reverb, uses multi-timbral LA synthesiser.
Supplier: Roland
Tel: 081 847 5665 (UK)

SoundBlaster 16 ASP
System: PC/MPC
Description: 16-bit sound card.
Supplier: West Point Creative
Tel: 0743 236605 (UK)

SoundBlaster Pro
System: PC/MPC
Description: Stereo 8-bit sound card, controller for Panasonic CR-521 CD-ROM drive. Able to sample stereo sound up to 22.05 KHz, mono up to 44.1 KHz. Supplied with bundled software, including Voice Editor.
Supplier: West Point Creative
Tel: 0743 236605 (UK)

Appendix H

Selected Multimedia and CD-ROM titles, publishers and suppliers

MPC and PC CD-ROM publishers and suppliers

CD Fiche Distributors Limited
Unit 4 Lloyds Court
Manor Royal
Crawley, West Sussex RH10 2XT. Tel: 0293 25271

Chadwyck Healey Limited
Cambridge Place
Cambridge CB2 1NR. Tel: 0223 311479

Future Office Systems Limited
Firs House
High Street
Whitchurch
Aylesbury, Bucks, HP22 4LL. Tel: 0296 641110

Microinfo Limited
PO Box 3
Omega Park
Alton, Hampshire, GU34 2PG. Tel: 0420 86848

Microsoft Limited
Excel House
Caversham Road
Reading, Berkshire, RG1 8LP. Tel: 0734 391123

Nimbus Information Systems
Wyastone Leys
Monmouth
Gwent NP5 3SR. Tel: 0600 890682

Optech Limited
East Street
Farnham
Surrey, GU9 7XX. Tel: 0252 714340

Sierra On-Line Limited (Entertainment software)
Unit 2, Technology Centre
Station Road
Theale
Reading, Berkshire, RG7 4AA. Tel: 0734 303322

The Software Toolworks
60 Leveroni Court
Novato
CA 94949, USA. Tel: (415) 883 3000

The Times Network Systems Ltd
Priory House
St. John's Lane
London EC1M 4BX. Tel: 071 782 7143

Selected PC CD-ROM and MPC titles

CD-ROMs in Print
System: PC
Publisher: Meckler

Cinemania
(Movie directory)
System: MPC
Publisher: Microsoft

Coate's Impressionism
System: PC & Macintosh
Publisher: Quanta Press

Composer Quest
System: PC and MPC
Publisher: Dr T's

Compton's Multimedia Encyclopedia
System: PC
Publisher: Britannica Software

Comstock Desktop Photography
System: PC and Macintosh
Publisher: Comstock

Educorp CD-ROM 5.0 (Public domain software compilation)
System: Macintosh
Publisher: Educorp

Educorp Clip-art CD-ROM
System: Macintosh
Publisher: Educorp Inc

Electronic Encyclopedia
System: PC and Macintosh
Publisher: Grolier Electronic Publishing

Electronic Home Library
System: PC
Publisher: World Library Inc

Encarta (Multimedia encyclopedia)
System: MPC
Publisher: Microsoft

Eric (Bibliographic database of literature about education)
System: PC and Macintosh
Publisher: Silver Platter

European Business Guide
System: PC
Publisher: Philips/BIP

Financial Times on CD-ROM
System: PC
Publisher: Chadwyck Healey

GCSE Mathematics
System: PC
Publisher: Top Class Technology

Library of the Future Second Edition
System: PC
Publisher: World Library Inc

Mammals: The Illustrated Encyclopedia
System: PC
Publisher: The Software Toolworks

Microsoft Encarta Multimedia Encyclopedia
System: MPC
Publisher: Microsoft

Microsoft Office
System: Macintosh
Publisher: Microsoft
Tel: 0734 391123

Microsoft Programmers Library
System: PC
Publisher: Microsoft
Tel: 0734 391123

Microsoft Works for Windows: Multimedia Edition
System: MPC
Publisher: Microsoft
Tel: 0734 391123

Microsoft Bookshelf for Windows
System: MPC
Publisher: Microsoft
Tel: 0734 391123

Microsoft Musical Insruments
System: MPC
Publisher: Microsoft
Tel: 0734 391123

Mozart 'The Dissonant'
System: Macintosh
Publisher: Voyager

Mozart 'The Magic Flute'
System: Macintosh
Publisher: Warner New Media

Multimedia Beethoven: The Ninth Symphony
System: MPC
Publisher: Microsoft
Tel: 0734 391123

Musical Instruments of the World
System: MPC
Publisher: Microsoft
Tel: 0734 391123

NERIS (National Educational Resources Information Services)
System: PC, Macintosh and Archimedes
Publisher: Neris

Oxford Textbook of Medicine
System: PC
Publisher: Oxford University Press

PC Select (contains 170 leading US computer magazines)
System: PC
Distributor: Parkway Goron
Tel: 0491 875386

Schubert: 'The Trout Quintet'
System: Macintosh
Publisher: Voyager

Shakespeare on Disc
System: PC
Publisher: CMC Research

Shareware Gold
System: PC
Publisher: Quanta Press

Space Series - Apollo
System: PC and Macintosh
Publisher: Quanta Press

Stravinsky 'The Rite of Spring'
System: Macintosh
Publisher: Voyager

The 1992 Time Magazine Compact Almanac
System: PC
Publisher: Compact Publishing

The CD-ROM Directory
System: PC
Publisher: TFPL

The Front Page News
System: PC and Macintosh
Publisher: Wayzata

The Guardian
System: PC
Publisher: Chadwyck Healey

The Independent
System: PC
Publisher: FT Profiles

The KGB World Factbook
System: PC and Macintosh
Publisher: Quanta Press

The Illustrated Shakespeare
System: PC
Publisher: Animated Pixels

The Multimedia Encyclopedia of Mammalian Biology
System: PC
Publisher: McGraw Hill

The New England Journal of Medicine
System: PC and Macintosh
Publisher: CMC Research

The Northern Echo
System: PC
Publisher: North of England Newspapers

The Orchestra, The Instruments Revealed
System: Macintosh
Publisher: Warner New Media

The Times & Sunday Times
System: PC, Macintosh and Archimedes (DOS emulation)
Publisher: TTNS

The Software Toolworks Illustrated Encyclopedia
System: PC
Publisher: The Software Toolworks

Appendix I

Miscellaneous multimedia contacts

Francis Media (Anglo-Dutch multimedia consultants & technical writers)
106 Swansea Road
Garden Village
Gorseinon
Swansea SA4 4HQ, UK
Tel: 0792 899149; 0792 897855
Cix: fmedia@cix

BIMA (British Interactive Multimedia Association)
Jane Callaghan
6 Washingley Road
Folksworth
Peterborough, PE7 3SY, UK
Tel: 0733 242370

EMAP Maclaren (Publishers of Multimedia magazine and Audio Visual magazine)
PO Box 109,
Maclaren House
Scarbrook Road
Croydon
Surrey CR9 1QH, UK
Tel: 081 688 7788

Glossary

1.2 Mbytes: Approximate formatted data capacity of standard IBM, high density, 5.25'' floppy disk.

1.44 Mbytes: Approximate formatted data capacity of standard high-density, IBM and Apple double-sided, 3.5'' floppy disk.

4:3: Typical aspect ratio of computer display *(See Aspect Ratio).*

24-bit Graphics: Computer images generated using 24 bits. Red, green and blue are each represented by eight bits, giving 256 tones of each, which in turn leads to over 16.7 million (256 * 256 * 256) colours. Near photographic-quality images possible.

32-bit Graphics: Computer images generated using 32 bits. Red, green and blue each represented by eight bits, giving 256 tones of each, which in turn leads to over 16.7 million (256 * 256 * 256) colours. Additional eight bits used to control transparency (Alpha Channel in Apple parlance). Photographic quality images possible. Apple Macintosh remembered as first platform upon which capability became commercially available.

4GL: (Fourth Generation Language) Programming environment which does not require programming code on a line by line basis.

50 Hz: Field rate yielding 25 frames or picture-updates per second in accordance with PAL video/broadcast standard.

60 Hz: Field rate yielding 30 frames or picture updates per second in accordance with the NTSC video/broadcast standard.

66.7 Hz: Frame rate of Apple Macintosh graphics.

150 Kbytes/sec: Average user data transfer rate of most Mode 1 CD-ROM *(See Data Transfer Rate)*. Also, user data transfer rate of CDI Form 1 disc.

170.2 Kbytes/sec: Average user data transfer rate of CDI Form 2 disc *(See Data Transfer Rate)*.

171 Kbytes/sec: Average user data transfer rate of Mode 2 CD-ROM *(See Data Transfer Rate)*.

171.1 Kbytes/sec: Data transfer rate of audio CD encoded according to the Red Book standard.

286: 16-bit 80286 processor, launched by Intel in 1982. Inexpensive, large user base in the form of the IBM PC AT, but antiquated design by modern standards.

360 Kbytes: Approximate formatted data capacity of standard IBM, 40 track, single-density, double-sided, 5.25'' floppy disk. Most widely used distribution medium for computer software throughout much of the Eighties.

386: Intel 80386 processor, launched in 1985, comprises a 32-bit data bus. Relatively expensive because solely manufactured by Intel (1991). However, Advanced Micro Devices hope to break legal monopoly (1991).

386sl: Intel 386 processor designed and developed for laptops, essentially a 386SX variant, but consumes less power and has built-in memory cache. A static design, it does not require the constant refreshing associated with the 386SX. It is used in conjunction with the 82360SL companion chip which yields the Industry Standard Architecture (ISA) bus. The partnership forms basis for complete system.

386SX: Intel 80386SX processor, launched in 1988 as an inexpensive route to 386 processing.

400 Kbytes: Approximate standard data capacity of Apple 3.5'' disk.

486: Intel 80486 processor, launched 1989, 32-bit with integral co-processor/math feature.

486SX: Launched in 1991, the 486SX is an inexpensive route to 486 processing. Many observers believe it to be a response to the Am386. The 486SX lacks an FPU, which takes the form of an additional chip (80487SX).

525 Line: Number of horizontal scan lines incorporated in conventional television broadcasting according to the NTSC standard used in the US and Japan *(See NTSC)*.

527.3 Mbytes: User data capacity of one hour, Mode 1 CD-ROM disc and Form 1 CDI disc.

598.4 Mbytes: User data capacity of one hour, Form 2 CDI disc.

602 Mbytes: User data capacity of one hour, Mode 2 CD-ROM disc.

625 Line: Number of horizontal scan lines incorporated in PAL and SECAM broadcast television standard - prevalent in most other countries outside the US and Japan.

720 Kbytes: Approximate formatted data capacity of a standard IBM, double-density, double-sided, 3.5'' floppy disk.

800 Kbytes: Approximate formatted data capacity of Apple 3/2'' disk.

880 Kbytes: Formatted data capacity of a 3.5'' disk for the Commodore Amiga family of computers.

1,024: 1,024 bytes = 1 Kilo byte (Kbyte). 1,024 Kbytes = 1 Mega byte (Mbyte).

8859-1: Shorthand for ISO 8859-1 standard Latin character set.

9660: Shorthand for ISO 9660 standard CD-ROM discs *(See ISO 9660).*

2,048 bytes: User data in Mode 1 CD-ROM data block. Also, CDI user data of Form 1 sector.

2,324 bytes: CDI user data in Form 2 sector.

2,336 bytes: User data in Mode 2 CD-ROM data block. Also, usable bytes per sector (according to Red Book) on CD-DA.

2,352 bytes: Total data capacity of single, standard CD-ROM data block, or one CDI sector.

A-Level audio: CDI audio quality level equivalent to first play of a vinyl disc under optimum conditions, minus noise caused by static and physical stylus contact. A more compact representation of audio CD data, (in stereo) it consumes half the data capacity, thus transfer occupies half data channel leaving room for other multimedia elements such as video, computer graphics and text. Mono A-Level audio data is twice as compact as stereo A-Level audio data.

Absolute Addressing: Disc address of each data block in minutes:seconds:blocks *(See Chapter 2).*

Access Time: Time between data request and actual retrieval using data storage device. Hard disk and CD-ROM access times are measured in ms and are a functions of electromechanical architecture.

ActionMedia 750 Capture Board: Intel Capture Board built around the Digital Video Interactive (DVI) i750 chip set, used to compress images, video and audio data *(See DVI).*

ActionMedia 750 Delivery Board: Intel Delivery Board built around the DVI (Digital Video: Interactive) chip set, used to decompress audio and video data - laid using the 750 Capture Board - from digital storage device (with SCSI interface). The digital storage device is most often a CD-ROM drive *(See DVI).*

ADC: (Analogue to Digital Convertor) Used to convert continuously varying analogue signal into digital form. Accuracy depends upon the number of output bits and sampling rate. Used to digitise analogue audio. Also used to interface joy-sticks and other input devices which interpret motion in terms of varying resistance.

ADPCM: (Adaptive Delta Pulse Code Modulation) Process by which an analogue signal is converted into digital form. Development of Delta Modulation, which compares successive samples of analogue signal to generate digital equivalent and is unable to handle large transients reasonably well. The sampling rate influences how effectively sharply varying analogue signals are accurately digitised. ADPCM accommodates large transients in analogue signal more accurately due to the quantisation steps of digital output being varied in response to variation of input signal. Used in CDI.

Aftertouch: Keyboard which is sensitive to firmness of touch, ie musically, amplitude is increased by pressing harder on key(s).

AI: (Artificial Intelligence) Term used to describe the use of a system to emulate human decision making and learning abilities. An expert system, for example, is regarded as a form of artificial intelligence. It is believed that massively parallel systems will unleash and emulate many human-like thought processes. Neural networks represent a key area.

Algorithm: Collective name describing vehicular component of problem solving process. It can be a program or series of steps defining course of action which yields what is regarded to be an ultimate solution.

Alpha Channel: Apple terminology for additional 8-bit data channel on 32-bit colour system which provides control over transparency of pixels, thus facilitating numerous video effects.

Am386: Advanced Micro Device (AMD) processor compatible with Intel 386, 386SX and 386SL. It can be run at up to 40 MHz. The true Intel 386 operates up to 33 MHz.

Amplitude: Volume of sound - or magnitude of digital or analogue signal.

Analogue: Signal which does not vary in precise preset steps, but may pass smoothly from one level of amplitude to another. Waveforms are used to represent analogue entities such as sound. For storage and processing using computers, analogue signals are converted into digital from using analogue to digital convertors (ADC) of which many variants exist, resulting in digitisation where a binary equivalent is generated *(See ADC and Digital).*

Analogue RGB: Method by which red, green and blue components are excited in accordance to individual (analogue) constantly varying voltages.

Animatic: Film or video representation of a production showing essential images only - motion picture equivalent of story board.

Apple Computer: Microcomputer manufacturer renowned for innovative designs and for consistently setting high standards later sought by competing companies. Co-founded by Steve Jobs, the company underwent a meteoric rise to becoming a heavyweight multinational in the Eighties. After beginning with the Apple Lisa - designed by Steve Wozniak - the launch of the highly successful Macintosh (Mac) computer in 1984 represented a significant point in its history. The Macintosh has since been refined into several versions and is an excellent platform for multimedia delivery and development. HyperCard is synonymous with the Macintosh and was to mark the beginning of a deserved reputation for suitability to multimedia. The association of the Macintosh with multimedia has been cultivated by numerous third-party manufacturers.

Apple Computer Human Interface Guidelines: Guidelines drafted by Apple Computer to promote consistency between different applications and programs, thus making them easier to use and learn in terms of user-interaction.

AppleTalk™: Network capability built in to Macintosh computers. Permits mixed-machine network making data interchangeable between different machines. Can be used with LocalTalk™ cabling to Token-Ring and Ethernet.

Appliance Controller: Generic name for a device through which a computer controls an appliance.

Applications Software: Software specifically developed for singular use, ie a relational database program provides the basis for a RDBMS (relational database management system), and therefore comes under the heading of applications software.

ASCII: (American Standard Code for Information Interchange) Standard code introduced to promote compatibility in terms of representation of characters and symbols. Originally consisted of 127 ASCII characters derived from seven bits (8 bits were not used in order to preserve the sign bit). Has since been extended into larger highly standardised character set.

Aspect Ratio: Width to height ratio of image or display. Scaling still or moving images proportionately requires maintenance of aspect ratio. The 640 by 480 pixel resolution possible using a Macintosh, and the 800 by 600 as well as 1,024 by 768 pixels resolution of a PC VGA partnership give an aspect ratio of exactly 4:3.

Attack: Rising amplitude of note or 'sequence', immediately after sounding.

Audio Block: Block on CD/CD-ROM used to store audio data. 2304 bytes of data in CDI audio sector, 2336 bytes in block of CD-DA.

Audio Data: Data resulting from the successful digitisation of analogue audio. Precise form is a function of standard or non-standard technique adopted.

Audio Sector/Block: Sector/block used to store audio data *(See audio block).*

Audio Signal: Electrical representation of sound waves, realised following amplification.

AudioSphere™: System/concept for the 3D rendering of audio in a virtual reality environment, producing sounds relative to user's location and sound source.

Authoring Language: High level Language for authoring multimedia, IV, hypertext or hypermedia material *(See HyperTalk).*

Authoring: Process of developing multimedia material.

Authoring System: Hardware platform and software required for the development of multimedia material, should also provide a means through which resultant material can be submitted to company for mastering and replication.

Authoring Tool: Program which permits the creation of multimedia or IV material. HyperCard is an authoring tool, which also provides an appropriate environment for multimedia delivery.

AVC: (Audio Visual Connection) IBM multimedia authoring software which runs in the DOS 4.0, OS/2 Standard Edition and OS/2 Extended Edition environments.

AVI: (Audio Video Interleave) Windows file format used for storing interleaved video clips and sound bites.

AYLI ("aily") Environment: (As you left it) Program or system which regurgitates on power up or activation of software, programs, text and information exactly as left following: i) a previous session of interaction, ii) after exiting an application, ii) or switching off system.

Backdrop: Background image. In CDI a backdrop image plane becomes totally visible when all other image planes are transparent.

Backtracking: In hypertext and hypermedia, process of retracing a user's path. It can be seen on numerous other applications, including Microsoft Windows 3.0, used as a means of retracing a complex series of menu selections. HyperCard's Recent command also permits backtracking.

Base Case Disc (CDI): Disc playable on Base Case System *(See Base Case System).*

Base Case System (CDI): Minimal implementation of the CDI Full Functional Specification.

BER: (Bit Error Rate) Measurement of how error-free the storage or transmission of data is. Typically expressed as the average number of bits in which one bit-error will occur. CD-ROM and CDI have appropriate error detection and correction capability *(See Mode 1 and Form 1).* In Mode 1 discs, 4 bytes are reserved for error detection and 276 bytes are reserved for error correction. Calculation of BER demands repetitive testing *(See Read Error Rate).*

Bit: A single binary digit '1' or '0'.

Bit Error Rate: *(See BER).*

Bit Map: Images or text represented by pixel data which defines each pixel are said to be 'bit mapped'. Pixel data is referred to as bit map. Can provide intricate control over graphics resulting in high quality *(See Bit-Mapped Display).* Image files tend to be large *(See Image Compression).*

Bit-Mapped Display: Graphic controller and display partnership, where pixel data representing each pixel is stored in memory *(See Bit Map).*

Block: CD/CD-ROM tracks are separated into blocks of 2,352 bytes.

Block Address: *(See Absolute Addressing)*

BNC: (BayoNet class of Connector) Connector consisting of round socket and plug which are locked together with a twist; invented by the engineers Neill and Concelman at Bell Laboratories.

Boolean Logic: AND, OR, NOR, NAND and NOT are Boolean operators. Boolean algebra was invented by George Boole, Irish mathematician.

Bookmark: Marker inserted in a document so as it can be revisited.

Broadcast Quality: Video said to approximate that used on broadcast television. In the light of HDTV, however, current broadcast quality video is comparatively crude.

Browse (browsing): Following the intricate paths through an information structure (hypermedia) at micro level.

Browser: Retrieval system, program module, or mode of operation which facilitates browsing.

Bug: Hardware or software error/fault in system/program. Originally coined by Grace Hopper - computer pioneer and inventor of Cobol and did much work in developing valve computers and high-level languages. Using the Harvard Mk 2 computer she discovered a hardware fault caused by a moth caught between the contacts of a relay. 'Debugging' the system, the unfortunate moth was entered in the computer's log at 15.45, 9 September 1945 - which is now at the Naval Museum, Virginia.

Burst Mode Transfer: Data transfer rate from CD-ROM many times greater than the average data transfer rate of 150 Kbytes/sec (Mode 1) or 171 Kbytes/sec (Mode 2), sustainable for a limited period of data transfer. Can be assumed faster over SCSI bus. Typically in the Mbyte range.

Button: Active area on screen, usually iconic representation of option, feature or application, and responsive to mouse selections, or to touch.

Byte: Piece of digital information eight bits in length.

C: General purpose high-level programming language. A structured programming language, it provides a means for developing programs with a logical and rigourous structure. It is also recursive permitting routines to be invoked from within themselves. Commercial implementations facilitating object oriented programming (OOP) exist (See OOP). Most popular C implementations for the PC come from Borland, and cheaper packages are available from Zortech.

Cache Controller: Sophisticated hard disk controller comprising on-board processor and, typically, several Mbytes of fast access RAM - which is usually expandable. It speeds up read/write operations by using its on-board RAM as an intermediate data store between disk and system memory. Based upon which data is most often requested, a caching algorithm estimates which portions of hard disk should reside in on-board RAM, thus making it instantly available. The ingenuity of this technique simply takes advantage of the inescapable fact that a small percentage of disk data is rewritten and accessed most frequently. The decision making process which is completely insulated from the system processor fuels the view that it is an 'intelligent controller'. Cache controllers are the most expensive of all variants, and in terms of random access will out-perform others.

CAD: (Computer Aided Design) Use of computer to assist in: two and three dimensional design, mathematical aspect of design process, producing computer models and simulations. Key areas include automotive design, architectural design, electronics design and others. AutoCad is possibly the best known CAD program for the PC. Such is the intense arithmetic nature of graphical CAD through matrix transformations, PCs fitted with co-processors, or 486-based, are often essential.

CAL: (Computer-assisted Learning) Educational/training computer program with which the student/pupil interacts. Research clearly indicates that increased recall is reaped through such interaction.

CASE: (Computer-aided software engineering) Programming tools which do not require intimate knowledge of programming language.

CAV: (Constant Angular Velocity) Reference to a disc that rotates at a fixed rate. Discs (such as CAV laserdiscs and vinyl) are not encoded at uniform density - data increases in density converging upon the centre.

CBT: (Computer-based Training) Use of computer as a source of training. Interactive video and multimedia are often used in CBT.

CCITT: (Committee Consultitif International Telegraphique et Telephonique) Standards organisation concerned mainly with communications.

CD: (Compact Disc) Optical disc developed for the storage of digital audio. Evolved into many variants such as CD-ROM, CDI and CD-V.

CD Player: Consumer device for playing audio CDs encoded according to the Red Book standard *(See CD-DA)*.

CD Graphics: Used in Japan, method by which text, graphics and animations can be recorded in subcode channels of CD.

CD-DA: (Compact Disc - Digital Audio) Also known as Red Book Standard, audio CD used in music industry since October 1982 (developed by Philips and Sony Corporation *(See Red Book standard)*.

CDI: (Compact Disc-Interactive) Multimedia system developed by Philips *(See Chapter 3)*.

CDI Base Case Player: Minimal implementation of a CDI player/decoder as set out in the CDI Full Functional Specification.

CDI Sector: Tracks on CDI disc consist of sectors 2,352 bytes long. User data yielded is a function of Form. Form 1 yields 2,048 bytes, and Form 2 gives 2,324 bytes.

CDI Track: CDI data track with Form 2 sectors only.

CD-R: (CD-Recordable): CD drive capable of writing to blank discs, usually in a variety of different formats, such as PhotoCD, XA, CDI and CD-ROM (See Chapter 2).

CD-ROM: (Compact Disc - Read Only Memory) Universal distribution medium. Announced in 1983 it is typically a 12 cm diameter optical disc offering data capacity in the hundreds of Mbytes range *(See Chapter 2)*. Includes spiralling track some three miles long. Developments include an eight cm version as well as high capacity quad-density variants.

CD-ROM Drive: Device for reading CD-ROM discs, can be portable, stand-alone or integral to computer/multimedia system. Modern drives with the exception of CDI are able to read Mode 1 and Mode 2 discs in the ISO 9660 and HSG formats, as well as audio CDs. All high specification variants read audio CDs.

CD-ROM Data Block: Standard 2,352 byte blocks forming the CD-ROM format. User data yielded by each block is a function of Mode of operation *(See Mode 1 and Mode 2)*.

CD-ROM XA: (Compact Disc - Read Only Memory eXtended Architecture) Published by Microsoft, Philips and Sony in March 1988, permits CDI title to be delivered using a conventional desktop computer with installed CD-ROM drive and CD-ROM XA decoder - initially appeared for the PC.

CD-RTOS: (Compact Disc - Real-Time Operating System) Philips' name for enhanced OS/9 operating system *(See OS/9)*. 100% downwardly compatible with OS/9. Consists of libraries, CD-RTOS kernel, managers and drivers. Libraries ensure that high-level commands are able to implement frequently required operations such as I/O functions and synchronisation in CDI systems. The CD-RTOS kernel is the shell and is an enhanced OS/9 variant. Managers accommodate graphics devices, input devices, audio processing devices, disc I/O and more. Drivers provide the software interface between hardware variants of various kinds and the CDI system.

CDTV: (Commodore Dynamic Total Vision) Consumer multimedia system based on Amiga connected to CD-ROM drive. World's first consumer multimedia system launched in 1991. Low-cost, drives a conventional television receiver, and includes an ISO 9660 CD-ROM drive which supports Mode 1 and Mode 2 operation.

CD-V Player: (Compact Disc - Video Player) Device able to play CD-V and CD-DA discs.

CD-V single: (Compact Disc - Video) Developed by Philips, mixed format CD. Stores 6 minutes motion video with digital stereo and 20 minutes of CD-DA audio. 18,000 stills stored in LaserVision format, or 80 Mbytes of data.

CED: (Capacitance Electronic Disc) In the early days of videodisc, research originally centred around using a high speed vinyl disc system. This led to an unacceptable ware problem of both stylus and disc, and was solved using CED. CED reduced friction by using the disc and stylus as a pair of capacitor plates. The charge varies according to grooves in disc.

Chunk-based: Hypertext, hypermedia or multimedia where links are implanted at the macro-level. Complete documents, 'cards' or 'chunks' are linked.

CLUT: (Colour Look-up Table) - Table in memory used to store colour palette.

CLUT animation: Method of animation by repeatedly changing data in colour look-up table.

CLV: (Constant Linear Velocity) - CD-ROM drives operate in CLV mode where the read head passes above spiralling track at uniform velocity. Disc is encoded at uniform density, thus disc spins faster as read head converges on centre.

Coaxial Cable (Coax): Cable arrangement where signal-carrying conductors are surrounded by a braided sheath (usually copper or aluminium) which eliminates electromagnetic interference. Standard cable for connecting TV receivers to aerials and VCRs.

Codec: (Compression Decompression)- Standard compression method.

Cognition: Thought process viewed at the macro level.

Colour Cycling (CDI): Changing from one colour lookup table to another, thus changing image colours without altering pixel data *(See CLUT)*.

Combi Player: Optical disc drive capable of playing both video disks and audio CDs.

Compatibility: Product of standardisation, determines how interchangeable medium, program, data or system is. For example, the medium of audio CD is compatible with all audio players, CDI players and high spec CD-ROM drives.

Compiled: Process by which source code of high-level language is translated into machine-executable form ie, machine code. Program need only be compiled once.

Compiler: Program or program module able to convert source code into machine-executable code. Unlike interpreter which attaches precise code to high-level statements each time program is run, a compiler produces machine-executable object code once. Inexpensive to develop, BASIC interpreters were widely used in the microcomputer industry in the Eighties.

Composite Monitor: Monitor which accepts composite video signal like that used in television broadcasting *(See Composite Video)*.

Composite Signal: Signal where brightness, chrominance and synchronisation information are combined. Used in conventional television broadcasting *(See CVBS)*.

Composite Video: Video signal where brightness, chrominance and sync information are combined.

Compressed Image: Image after compression through hardware and/or software means.

Compression: Method by which computer data of any kind (often image data) is scaled down, eventually consuming less storage space and providing a means for increased data transfer rate *(See RLC, DCT, DVI, JPEG and MPEG).*

Compression Ratio: Ratio relating size of a data file before and after compression.

Computer Graphics (CG): Images generated, manipulated and stored using computer system. Crude images possible using character-graphics, extensively used in computer games owing to the speed at which resulting sprites can be manipulated. Bit-mapped graphics can provide photographic quality images, but give rise to large image files, of which numerous formats exist.

Controller: Generic name for a hardware component which controls a peripheral device, such as a disk drive, CD-ROM drive or monitor.

Co-processor: Additional processor dedicated to a certain type of processing. IBM machines often come with sockets for 8087, 80287, 80387SX and 80387 co-processors, which implement floating point arithmetic operations. Co-processors must by matched to the system processor, where a 16 MHz 386SX will require a 16 Mhz 387SX. Useful and often essential for applications dependent upon a great number arithmetic operations.

Courseware: Generic term for material used in education/training.

CPU: (Central Processing Unit) *(See Processor).*

CRC: (Cyclic Redundancy Check) Error detection scheme used on CD as well as other storage devices.

Cursor: Typically represented by flashing line or box; indicates X-Y position of point of input (or interaction) on screen. Using a word processor, it indicates the row and column position where text can be erased, overwritten or inserted. Also used to make menu selections. In DTP, CAD and graphics packages, cursor plays the role of menu selections, drawing and dragging screen objects.

Cursor Plane: In CDI, small graphical image that can be made visible or invisible and can be moved over other image planes. Used for pointing purposes (pointer/cursor).

Cut: Video or film technique when video footage is switched to another sequence - can include still video images.

Cut and Paste: Process by which section of a screen image is removed (cut) and implanted (pasted) elsewhere in the image or into another image.

CVBS: (Composite Video Broadcast Signal) Standard colour, composite video broadcast signal *(See Composite Signal).*

Cyclic Redundancy Check: *(See CRC).*

Daisy Chain: Method of uniting a number of CD-ROM drives so as to combine overall data capacity. The number of drives which may be linked is a function of drives used.

DAT: (Digital Audio Tape) World-wide standard for digital audio tape recording, covering physical attributes and encoding. Noticeably smaller than Compact Cassettes, DAT cassettes offer two hours of continuous digital audio play-back. Conventional Compact Cassettes are encoded horizontally using a fixed magnetic head. Head current induces an analogue magnetic signal on tape, via a head gap. DAT cassettes are encoded diagonally using twin rotary head. Like CD-DA, CIRC error correction ensures high sound quality and long life.

Data Capacity: Amount of user data that can be stored on CD-ROM or other DSM. Length of a CD-ROM in minutes and data block size in terms of user data, provides a means of calculating disc capacity with pin-point accuracy. For example, consider the following simple formula:

*User data capacity = disc length (seconds) * blocks read per second * usable block data*

Or, using CDI discs:

*User data capacity = disc length (seconds) * sectors read per second * usable sector data*

Applying this formula to calculate the precise data capacity of a 65 mins, 12 secs, Mode 1 or CDI Form 1 disc gives:

User data capacity = 3,912 * 75 * 2,048 bytes = 600,883,000 bytes = 573 Mbytes

The capacity of a 65 mins, 12 secs Mode 2 CD-ROM disc:

User data capacity = 3,912 * 75 * 2,336 bytes : = 685,382,000 bytes = 653.6 Mbytes

The data capacity of a 65 mins, 12 secs, CDI Form 2 disc:

User data capacity = 3,912 * 75 * 2,324 bytes = 681,861,000 bytes = 650.2 Mbytes

Data Transfer Rate (Average user data transfer rate): Rate at which data is transferred from CD-ROM/CDI drive. Typically, it is standardised on old-fashioned drives at either 150 Kbytes/sec or circa 171 Kbytes/sec.

Average user data transfer rate can be calculated using the following simple formula:

*Average user data transfer rate = blocks/sec * user data/block*

Or in CDI terms:

*Average user data transfer rate = sectors/sec * user data/sector*

In Mode 1 and CDI Form 1 operation:

Average user data transfer rate = 75 * 2,048 = 153,600 bytes/sec = 150 Kbytes/sec

Turning to Mode 2 discs, a noticeable improvement is brought about through increased user block data:

Average user data transfer rate = 75 * 2,336 = 175,200 bytes/sec = 171 Kbytes/sec

CDI Form 2 discs:

Average user data transfer rate = 75 * 2,324 = 174,300 bytes/sec = 170.2 Kbytes/sec

Database: Electronic information system offering data storage and retrieval. *Relational* databases are used to store tabular information in the form of records, and useful versions are able to generate graphs. Popular PC relational databases include Borland Paradox, dBase, Q & A and DataEase. *Text* databases are used to store documents such as articles and even complete books. Documents can be indexed where the user-interface simply allows users to search for documents which contain target words, phrases or sentences.

DCC: (Digital Compact Cassette) - Audio distribution medium developed by Philips, and launched in 1991. Players able to play both DCC and conventional Compact Cassette are commercially available. This dual compatibility is regarded a significant advantage.

DCT: (Discrete Cosine Transform) - Highly effective lossy image-compression technique which converts image data from the spatial domain into the frequency domain. It is combined with RLC and Huffman coding within the JPEG algorithm.

DDE: (Dynamic Data Exchange) - Program/feature that is able to import and export data in real-time.

Digital: Digital devices such as computers process and store data in the form of ones and zeros, which are represented by different voltage levels. In a positive logic representation, 'one' might be '+5' volts and zero '0' volts. This lowest of levels at which computers operate is known as machine code. Binary arithmetic and Boolean algebra (named after Irish mathematician George Boole) permit mathematical representation. Boolean algebra and Karnaugh maps used widely for minimisation of logic algebraic expressions. Though digital signals exist at two levels (one or zero), an indeterminate state is possible.

Disc Physical Format: Format in terms of blocks/sectors for storing data on disc.

Disc Replication: Manufacture of discs copied from master disc.

Disc Storage: Use of disc (optical, magnetic or otherwise) to store digital data.

Dot Pitch: Distance between physical pixels on monitor screen, indicating clarity of picture and maximum resolution supported.

Double Resolution: CDI double resolution of 720 by 240 pixels using NTSC, and 768 by 280 in PAL/SECAM.

Doublespace: Real-time data compression algorithm built into MS-DOS 6.0. Depending upon the file types stored on a hard disk it theoretically doubles disk data capacity. There are numerous other so-called on-the-fly data compression programs on the market for both the PC and Apple Macintosh. These include Stacker (Stac electronics), SuperStor, DoubleDisk (Vertisoft), XtraDrive (IIT), Double Density (Abacus), AutoDoubler (Fifth Generation Systems), Stuffit SpaceSaver (Aladdin Systems), SuperDisk (Alysis Software), TimesTwo (Golden Triangle Computers). There is also a third party utility, SPACEMANager (Vertisoft), that helps you manage MS-DOS doublespace drives.

DR-DOS: (Digital Research - Disk Operating System) Operating system based upon Digital Research CPM (Control Program for Microcomputers). Minor Deviations from MS-DOS. DR-DOS 5.0, for example, is slightly incompatible with MS-DOS 4.01 and MS-DOS 5.0. DR-DOS 6.0 is the most recent version (1993), which does not feature a built-in real-time compression algorithm as found in MS-DOS 6.0 under the name DoubleSpace. This roughly doubles the data capacity of storage media.

DV-MCI: (Digital Video - Media Control Interface) - Extension to MCI that permits delivery of digital video.

DVI: (Digital Video Interactive) - Video compression and decompression technology for the AT and MCA bus, thus aimed at PC ATs and PS/2 systems (beginning with model 50).

E-mail: (Electronic-mail) - Transmission and reception of textual material (and occasionally visuals) via electronic means. Typically, a computer fitted with a modem (Modulator Demodulator) is used for transmission and reception over the telephone network.

EAPROM: (Electrically Alterable Programmable Read Only Memory) - Electronic memory which can be erased electrically.

Electronic Publishing: Vague term used to describe information made available through electronic means.

Electronic Storyboard: Computer equivalent of storyboard, used for the development of multimedia material. Provides cost-effective means of early prototyping when, for instance, only salient images have been, or need be, gathered. Depending upon computer software used, can present blinkered view, where an overall picture is difficult to grasp. For example, depending upon complexity, pinning a storyboard on wall(s) imparts immediate overview of meaningful paths and possible user interaction and so forth.

EPROM: (Erasable Programmable Read Only Memory) - Electronic memory which can be erased by subjecting chip to UV light. Once programmed transparent window is covered, making data permanent.

Expert Shell: Program able to support and interpret rule-base within expert system or KBS. Shell takes the form of a development tool for generating knowledge base. Rule-base can be loaded from other sources such as databases and word processors *(See KBS).*

Expert System: *(See KBS)*

Fifth Generation Language: Fifth generation languages are non-procedural (*See Procedural*). They are declarative in that actions are not implemented through fixed procedures. They are also known as AI languages and include PROLOG (PROgramming LOGic).

Firmware: Program or data stored using in ROM (See ROM, EPROM, PROM and EAROM). Firmware is thus involatile and permanent.

First Generation Language: First Generation computer languages require the entry of code in a hexadecimal form *(See Hex).* A collection of instructions entered in 'hex' represents a first generation language, and the system upon which it runs may be described as a first generation computer. Such languages are obsolete.

Fisheye Browser: In hypermedia, tool/feature which emphasises nodes in close proximity or of relevance.

Floppy disk: Magnetic storage media typically 3.5'' or 5.25'' diameter. Standard versions store between 360 Kbytes and 1.44 Mbytes for the IBM family of computers. Higher density drives exist, but are not standard. Some, however, are downwardly compatible with industry standard drives.

Form 1 and Form 2: Like CD-ROM blocks, both CD-ROM XA and CDI sectors are 2,352 bytes long - including headers, sync information, error detection and correction data. Both CD-ROM XA and CDI discs are Mode 2 variants. Form 1 sector yields

2,048 bytes user data. Form 2 sector yields 2,324 bytes user data *(See Data Capacity, Mode 1 and Mode 2, and Chapter 2).*

CD-ROM XA/CDI sector structure:	Form 1	Form 2
Synchronisation	12 bytes	12 bytes
Header	4 bytes	4 bytes
Subheader	8 bytes	8 bytes
User data	2048 bytes	2324 bytes

FPU: (Floating Point Unit) Math coprocessors such as the 80387 and 80287 are FPUs. The FPU can also be integrated into the processor chip itself (e.g. i80486).

Frame Grabber: Device used for digitising still or single frame of video. Once digitised, can be edited, manipulated and so forth. Video capture cards often comprise frame grabbing capability.

Genlock: Process of synchronising computer graphics with video images so as they can be mixed using 'genlock' device.

Graphic Controller: Device used to generate graphics and text. Also known as a graphics engine. A VGA card is a graphics engine, but is more commonly referred to as a graphics adapter or card. Standard IBM graphics cards include Monochrome Display Adapter (MDA), Colour Graphics Adapter (CGA), Enhanced Graphics Adapter (EGA), Video Graphics Array (VGA), Multi Colour Graphics Array (MCGA -used on PS/2 30) and 8514/A. The fastest graphics controllers are of the local bus variety. These connect more directly to the processor's data bus and are, therefore, unaffected by the slow data transfer rates that can be achieved over ISA, EISA or MCA buses.

Graphics Engine: *(See Graphic Controller)*

Graphics format: Image files may be produced according to a number of graphics formats, including GIF, PIC, TIFF, IMG, EPS and others. The efficiency of various image file formats in terms of the data capacity they consume tends to vary significantly. Perhaps one of the more efficient uncompressed image files formats is GIF.

Green Book standard: Alternative name for the CDI Full Functional Specification announced in June 1987, exactly one year after the first draft was issued.

GUI: (Graphical User Interface - 'gooey') - User interface consisting of icons, usually facilitating interaction via a mouse, resulting in minimal keyboard use. Sometimes referred to as front-end.

Hard disk: Magnetic mass storage device consisting of fixed disk. Removable versions are available but most are fixed. Storage capacities are increasing all the time *(See Chapter 3)*.

Hard disk controller: Device which interfaces a hard disk to a computer. Numerous commercial variants exist including MFM, RLL, ESDI, IDE and SCSI. Many track-buffered and all high performance cache controllers comprise on-board processors. All but those controllers incorporated into hard cards are able to support floppy disk drives, and usually possess multiple device capability. A standard SCSI controller will accommodate 7 hard disks. The addition of daughter-boards is often possible on sophisticated variants, offering further support for multiple devices.

HDTV: (High Definition Television) - Transmission of high quality television images beyond the PAL/SECAM and NTSC standards. Numerous technologies competing for standard in Europe, USA and Japan. MPEG highly significant to HDTV.

Hertz: Cycles or pulses per second. The Alternating Current (AC) supply in the UK is distributed at 50 Hz or cycles per second.

Hierarchal: Strict Hierarchy demands that objects are only accessible through a parent.

High Resolution: CDI high resolution equates to 720 by 480 in NTSC, and 768 by 560 in PAL/SECAM.

High Sierra Group: Standard for data storage on CD-ROM agreed in a meeting of industry representatives in 1985 at the High Sierra Hotel at Lake Tahoe, Nevada. Now part of CD-ROM folklore the meeting resulted in the High Sierra Group (HSG) standard, which introduced compatibility for the storage of alphanumeric data. Since built upon to become ISO 9660.

Himem: Highest user memory address in system.

Hit: Instant particular part of music or sound effect which coincides with relevant screen action in film, video or multimedia.

Horizontal market: Non-specialist market. For example, both the mass market and consumer market are horizontal.

Huffman Coding: Image-compression process which operates in the spatial domain - forms part of the JPEG algorithm.

Hyper: Meaning 'more than' or 'greater than', a fashionable prefix in computer terminology, and one which is particularly apt when considering hypertext and hypermedia.

HyperCard: Program for the Macintosh which permits the delivery and development of hypertext and hypermedia. Supplied with all Macintosh computers it represents a milestone in the development of multimedia.

Hypermedia: Extension of the hypertext concept where text is combined with images. The terms hypermedia and multimedia are often regarded as interchangeable. In French media circles the ludicrous and ridiculously extravagant term *hypermediatisation* was coined in 1991. It was used to describe the immediacy with which news began to be transmitted, brought about by SBLs (Satellite Broadcasting Links). With time normally required by the reporter to prepare an informed report sacrificed, the concept of resultant often confused reports became known as hypermediatisation.

HyperTalk: Language indigenous to HyperCard used for authoring hypertext/ hypermedia, or for conventional programming.

Hypertext: Term coined in the Sixties by Ted Nelson to describe the concept of linking textual information and presenting it in a non-linear fashion.

IBM: (International Business Machines) - Leading manufacturer of business computer systems. Launched the IBM PC in early Eighties that was to become an industry standard. Its successor, the PC AT was downwardly compatible, and it too became an industry standard. Introduced the Personal System/2 (PS/2) in mid 1987 incorporating the Micro Channel Architecture (MCA) bus for the first time. The IBM M-Motion Video Adapter enables video to be captured as VGA screens, and runs under both DOS and OS/2. Later versions operate in the Microsoft Windows environment. IBM is also engaged in DVI.

Icon: Graphical representation of an option, application or feature on screen. Sometimes referred to as a button, and selected by pointing and clicking a mouse, or through other means of user interaction.

IDE: (Intelligent Disk Electronics) - Disk controller (See Chapter 3) widely used on IBM PCs. Many motherboards have on-board IDE controllers. In standard form, at least two hard disks and two floppy disk drives are supported.

Image Compression: Means by which pixel data can be compressed *(See DCT and Image Processor).*

Image Format: Numerous image file formats exist for storing digital images, including PIC, TIFF, IMG, EPS, Amiga HAM and CompuServe GIF.

Image Processor: Processor specifically designed for image-compression purposes *(See Chapter 3).* Unlike conventional processor, it is usually designed to carry out specific matrix transformations at high speed.

Inmos: Chip manufacturer responsible for the innovative Transputer - a milestone in parallel processing history - and numerous other components including image compression processors and graphics chips. Once British-owned it was bought by the European Consortium SGS-Thompson in the late Eighties. Experienced problems in 1984 - 1985 as a result of Japan flooding world market with under-priced RAM. High value of sterling in 1990 caused further problems, as did recession of the early Nineties.

Input Device: An input device in the context of user-communication provides a means for user-interaction. A keyboard is an input device. Typically takes the form of mouse or remote control device. Touch-screens, track balls, joy sticks, control dials are all input devices. Often referred to as user-communication devices in earlier days.

Interchangeability: Generic term used to describe peripheral device or storage medium able to exist within more than one system type or operating system environment.

Interface device: Means of connecting peripheral devices to computer system, and consists of hardware and software.

Interlace: Horizontal lines of television image are drawn using an interlaced scan, in which one field draws odd lines, and another even lines - introduced to reduce picture flicker.

Interpreted: Interpreted language is one in which object code is generated from source code each time a program is run. Inexpensive microcomputers of the Eighties included BASIC interpreters.

Interpreter: Program which interprets a language (*See Interpreted*).

ISO: (International Standards Organisation) Organisation actively engaged in establishing standards in optics, image processing and video. Sponsors both JPEG and MPEG.

ISO 8859-1: Alphanumeric character set standard issued by the ISO.

ISO 9660: So successful was High Sierra, that it was built upon by the International Standards Organisation officially calling it ISO 9660. The ISO 9660 standard acted not only as a catalyst for the development of CD-ROM based applications, but stimulated drive manufacture also. Philips, Sony, Hitachi, NEC, Cumana and many others all produce ISO drives.

JPEG Algorithm: (Joint Photographics Experts Group Algorithm) - Standard devised by the JPEG covering still-image compression and decompression. Group sponsored by both ISO and CCITT *(See Chapter 3)*.

KBS: (Knowledge Based System) - Term which superseded expert system. Refers to program comprising a knowledge base often built up of rules, each comprising fact(s) and conclusion(s), ie IF disk drive light off THEN check ribbon cable. Confidence factors (in the form of percentages) can also be introduced where facts, conclusions, and deductions are appropriately weighted. Rule-base is exploited by inference engine which chains either backwards or forwards, yielding result(s). KBS can offer informed decision making skills, the effectiveness of which is a function of accuracy and comprehensiveness of rule- or knowledge- base. Knowledge engineer responsible for generating rule-base - proven to be complex and arduous process. Numerous applications include medicine, business, stock market, maintenance etc.

Kilo Byte (Kbytes, K): 1,024 bytes. Wrongly, often taken to mean 1000 bytes in accordance with the metric interpretation of Kilo. It is derived from a ten bit address bus thus giving access to 2^10 (1,024) memory locations.

Laptop Computer: Portable computer compact enough to be operable from a person's lap. Modern (circa A4 size) versions are often called notebook computers.

Laser: (Light Amplification by Stimulated Emission of Radiation) Device capable of producing coherent beam of light over a narrow wave length. Device is said to 'lase'. Solid state LED (Light Emitting Diode) laser together with lens (and mirror) assembly used to read all forms of compact disc.

LaserVision: Standard videodisc player and disc format developed by Philips. Manufactured by Philips and other manufacturers (e.g. Pioneer), now commonly used in IV applications as well as multimedia. Also consumer product.

LED: (Light Emitting Diode) Semiconductor device which emits visible light when excited electrically. Extensively used in all kinds of consumer electronics and computers, as power indicators and alphanumeric displays. Advantages over conventional filament bulbs include, near-infinite life span, incredibly durable, reliable, physically robust, easy to manufacture in different colours, low power consumption and inexpensive. Liquid Crystal Displays (LCDs) now taking over slightly for alphanumeric (LED) and graphical displays.

Link: Means of relating tables/files in relational database; used to associate nodes in hypertext and hypermedia, within which many different variants exist *(See Typed Link)*.

LinkWay: Hypermedia/hypertext authoring program for the IBM PC family of computers. Low-cost and relatively simple it was initially developed for the education sector. Produced by IBM.

Local bus: Method of connecting video cards, hard disk controllers directly to the processor's data bus, this overcoming the data transfer bottle-neck of ISA, EISA and MCA buses. Theoretically, local bus technology should permit the accommodation of expansion cards running, generally, at clock speeds equal to that of the processor's external data bus. Several local bus standards have emerged including VL-bus and Intel's PCI (Peripheral Component Interconnect).

LocalTalk™: Cabling system for Macintosh computer, supported by integral AppleTalk™.

Lomem: Lowest user memory address in system.

Lossy Compression: Image compression technique which is 'lossy' omits redundant pixel data - leads to sometimes unnoticeable loss of image quality.

Macintosh Classic (1991): Reincarnation of Apple Macintosh computer launched in 1984, supplied with HyperCard, integral mono monitor, based on Motorola 68000 running at 8 MHz, supports 1 to 4 Mbytes RAM, contains no expansion slots as standard, AppleTalk network capability and SCSI controller.

Macintosh IIsi: Apple Macintosh computer, supplied without monitor, drives colour or mono display as standard, HyperCard, 68030 - 20 MHz, 2 to 17 Mbytes of RAM, one expansion slot, AppleTalk network capability and SCSI controller.

Macintosh IIci: Apple Macintosh computer, supplied without monitor, drives colour or mono display as standard, HyperCard, 68030/68882 - 25 MHz, 5 to 8 Mbytes of RAM, three expansion slots, AppleTalk network capability and SCSI controller.

Macintosh IIfx: Apple Macintosh computer, supplied without monitor, drives colour or mono display as standard, HyperCard, 68030/68882 - 40 MHz, 4 to 8 Mbytes of RAM, six expansion slots, AppleTalk network capability and SCSI controller.

Macintosh LC: Apple Macintosh computer, launched in 1990, supplied without monitor, drives colour or mono display as standard, HyperCard, provides cost effective route to Macintosh II software by adding Apple IIe card to single expansion slot, 68020 - 16 MHz, 2 to 10 Mbytes of RAM, one expansion slot, AppleTalk network capability and SCSI controller, 40 Mbyte hard disk.

Macintosh Portable: Apple Macintosh portable computer, LCD display, CMOS 68000 - 16Mhz, 2 to 9 Mbytes RAM, one expansion slot, AppleTalk network capability and SCSI controller.

Macintosh SE/30: Like Macintosh Classic but with 68030/68882 - 8 MHz, 1 to 4 Mbytes RAM.

MacinTalk: Speech synthesis program for the Macintosh able to read text, and deliver sequences programmed using phonemes. Compatible with a number of other Macintosh programs.

Macintosh Computer: Launched by Apple Computer in 1984, now represents family of computers.

Macro level: Links which exist at the macro level relate relatively large documents or 'chunks'. They are said to exist at a high level, forming part of the chunk-based model of hypertext and hypermedia. Nelson refers to the macro level points as 'spans'. *(See Micro level).*

Magazine Drive: CD-ROM drive capable of reading a number of discs. Sometimes provides an inexpensive alternative to daisy chaining.

Mapi: (Messaging Application Programming Interface) Standard that permits dynamic media to successfully integrated into E-mail documents.

Mass Storage Device: Device used to store data. Can be assumed to be either magnetic, optical or magneto-optical.

Master Disc: Glass disc from which manufactured discs are produced.

Mastering System: System used to generate glass master disc.

MCI: (Media Control Interface) Integral to the Microsoft Windows multimedia extensions built into Windows 3.1 (and higher), consists of a suite of drivers together with command-set able to control connected multimedia devices such as sound cards, CD-ROM drives and so on. (See DV-MCI).

Media: Means through which information can be stored and communicated. Physical entities used to support or distribute information such as paper, magnetic disk and video tape.

Mega Byte (Mbytes, M): 1,024 Kbytes. Wrongly referred to as 1000 Kbytes. Derived from 20 address lines resulting in 2^20 (1,048,576) memory addresses.

Metaphor: Emulation or representation of process. A flat file database can be a card-box metaphor, for example. Equally, a GUI can be desktop metaphor.

MHz: (Mega Hertz) One million cycles or pulses per second. Commonly used to describe the clock speed of computers, thus providing indication of speed of operation. A 16 MHz machine will therefore yield 16 million clock cycles per second, and a single clock cycle will have a duration of $6.25 * 10^{-8}$ (1/16,000,000) secs.

Micon: (Motion Icon) Animated icon represented by a number of frames run in a continuous loop. Invented by Hans Peter Brondmo, these manifest more clearly the purpose, feature, application or program to which options lead.

Micro level: Links that occur at the micro level relate micro features, which can be single words or phrases. This low level approach yields advanced hypertext and hypermedia.

MIDI: (Musical Instrument Digital Interface) Industry standard providing a high degree of musical instrument (keyboard, for example) interchangeability. Covers hardware, cables, connectors, and data protocols (MIDI messages).

Mini Disc: Announced by Sony in 1991, a recordable audio distribution medium 2.5 ins diameter.

MIPS: (Million instruction Per Second) Standard unit for measuring raw processing power.

Mirroring: Function of hard disk controller, it involves data being written to more than one drive, and can improve data security.

Mode 1 and Mode 2: CD-ROM data structure supported by all modern drives. One hour Mode 1 disc yields 527 Mbytes data capacity and Mode 2 gives 602 Mbytes data capacity. Inexpensive drives offer Mode 1 and Mode 2 data transfer rates of 150 Kbytes/sec and 171.1 Kbytes/sec, respectively. A Mode 1 data block will yield just 2,048 bytes (2 Kbytes) user data, while Mode 2 capacitates 2.28 Kbytes user data. Tables 1 and 2 show the CD-ROM data block structure in Modes 1 and 2 respectively, illustrating Mode 1's lower user data due to demands imposed mainly by error correction.

<$tc>Table 1: Mode 1 block structure

Designation	**Size**	**Byte number**
Synchronisation	12 bytes	0 - 11
Header	4 bytes	12 - 15
User Data	2,048 bytes	16 - 2,063
Error detection	4 bytes	2,064 - 2,067
Space	8 bytes	2,068 - 2,075
Error correction	276 bytes	2,076 - 2,351

<$tc>Table 2: Mode 2 block structure

Designation	**Size**	**Byte number**
Synchronisation	12 bytes	0 - 11
Header	4 bytes	12 - 15
User Data	2,336 bytes	16 - 2351

Monitor: Based upon Cathode Ray Tube (CRT), Liquid Crystal Display (LCD), or Thin Film Transistor (TFT), in portable computers, a display devoid of tuner circuitry for accepting TV composite signals. Input is usually RGB or digital - 'machine specific' D-type socket is often included for the various IBM standards.

Mouse: X-Y input device typically consisting of two or three buttons, used for making selections and invoking various other program features. Can be cordless or physically connected to the system/computer. Was though to resemble 'mouse', and typically measures around 4'' by 2''. A hand-held pointing device, it is moved in an X-Y motion. Commonly used for DTP, CAD, art packages and GUIs. Numerous mouse devices exist including serial and parallel variants. Microsoft mouse represents industry standard.

MPC: (Multimedia PC) Standard issued by the Multimedia PC Marketing Council, of which Microsoft and Tandy are key members, which must be met if a PC is to wear the MPC™ badge (See Chapter 3).

MPEG Algorithm: (Motion Picture Experts Group Algorithm) Standard devised by the MPEG covering compression and decompression of digital moving pictures and associated audio. Group sponsored by ISO and CCITT.

MS-DOS: (Microsoft - Disk Operating System) Operating system based upon Digital Research CPM (Control Program for Microcomputers). Now a world-wide standard, it has evolved into numerous versions. DR-DOS by Digital Research and PC-DOS by IBM are also available.

Multifrequency Monitor: *(See Multisync Monitor).*

Multimedia: A broad, sometimes vague, and often misunderstood term which can be applied to a system or process which embodies and combines various kinds of conventional media. Modern multimedia can be assumed as comprising motion video *(See Chapter 1).*

Multimedia Authoring Tool: Software tool intended for the development of multimedia. Many require no programming skills.

Multimedia Delivery: Term used to describe the process of playing multimedia titles.

Multimedia Delivery System: System which may blend still or motion video, digitised photographic images, audio, synthesized sound, computer graphics and text, as well as provide real-time user-interaction and anything else a computer may offer. System must normally include computer, CD-ROM drive, appropriate display, video decompression capability and input device.

Multisync™ Monitor (Multifrequency or Multiscan Monitor): Monitor that can synchronise with various incoming signals. However, there are many technical implementations of the 'multisync monitor', the simplest of which will automatically synchronise with perhaps two horizontal frequencies and maybe two or three vertical frequencies. Professional versions are able to automatically synchronise with a range of horizontal and vertical frequencies. This is called the scanning range, and the greater it is, the greater the number of acceptable signal sources. Yet higher specification monitors economise on scan range, thus concentrating on the narrow band of professional graphic controllers beginning with VGA. Such monitors are often interchangeable.

Navigation: Process of moving between nodes via links in hypertext and hypermedia at macro level.

Non-Removable Medium: Storage medium which is fixed to system. Most hard disks are non-removable.

Normal Resolution: CDI normal pixel resolution of 360 by 240 in the NTSC system, and 384 by 280 in the PAL/SECAM system

Notebook: Portable computer with a footprint about the size of an A4 page. Most incorporate grey-scale LCDs. More expensive variants comprise colour TFT (Thin Film Transistor) displays.

NTSC: (National Television Standards Committee) American video/broadcast standard at 60 fields/30 frames per second on the 525 line system.

NuBus: Interface hardware and protocols on Macintosh II computers, enabling system expansion. NuBus slave boards operate under the control of another board or the system processor.

NVRAM: (Non-Volatile Random Access Memory) Re-writable electronic memory which preserves stored information following interruption of power supply. Useful for calendars, and other alterable information which must be preserved after a system is switched off.

On-board: Reference to device, or firmware integrated into the motherboard of a computer. Similarly, can equally refer to other electronic assembly.

OOP: (Object-oriented programming) Sometimes referred to as object-based programming. Central to the theme of object-oriented programming are classes, which brings the process of programming in line with the way we think about objects or *things* in the real world where, unconsciously, we place objects in classes. We know, for example, that cars, holiday chalets and computers are from different classes, but each time we see a car we don't ask ourselves: Now which class does a car belong to? Or why is it different from a holiday chalet? We know that it a member of the class vehicle because we have learned how it behaves, and that behaviour, with all its methods, is in our mind. We do not have to learn or consider an objects' behaviour each time we come in contact with it. For example, you know that you cannot drive the holiday chalet because of its behaviour, and the class to which it belongs. You know these things without having to, repeatedly, decide that a holiday chalet cannot be driven because it has no wheels, no axle, no engine and so on.

Object-oriented programs are much the same. Classes of objects are carefully defined early on in the program. If the class HoldayChalet were defined appropriately, we could not drive it by using the following command:

HolidayChalet.drive()

Only the correctly defined class, Car, could be made to drive using the command:

Car.drive()

Hierarchies form another important part of classes where, once again, like in the real world, classes are subdivided into further classes. This helps distinguish between, say, a sports car and a jeep. The jeep would be a member of the class OffRoadVehicles which is a member of the class, Cars, which in turn is a member of the class, Vehicles.

This additional information tells us that a sports car cannot be driven up a steep muddy slope etc. Everything in the real world is a member of a class, of which there are an infinite number.

Some Windows databases come with a number of in-built methods to choose from. These cover standard activities such as opening tables and forms, and even opening the Help window. This type of database building is achieved through a so-called 'pick and build' interface.

OLE: (Object Linking and Embedding): Process of linking two Windows applications by embedding an object from one into the other. The Windows application from which the object is embedded is termed the server application, while the application into which the object is embedded is termed the server. OLE Objects can be text, graphics, arithmetic or video.

Operating System (OS): Software used to manage the resources of a system and so provide an interface between user and system, as well between software and the system, and between the system and peripheral devices. The shell, user-interface or front-end is sensitive to a number of user-commands. Most operating systems are general purpose, with the exception of the Pick operating system which is aimed at database usage. Popular operating systems include MS-DOS, DR-DOS, OS/2 and Unix.

Optical Medium: Medium which is read using optical means. CD, CDI discs, CD-ROM, LaserVision (videodisc), CD-V are optical media.

Optical Storage Device: Storage device which uses optical media.

OS/2: (Operating System/2) Launched in mid 1987 to coincide with the release of the IBM PS/2 family of computers, it is a multitasking operating system able to run applications simultaneously, and is downwardly compatible with DOS. OS/2 is used in conjunction with Presentation Manager, a GUI. Relaunched in 1992 by IBM under the name OS/2 2.0 it is now a relatively successful 32-bit operating system. It is also able to run Microsoft Windows applications in either real of standard modes. Version 2.1 (mid 1993) included multimedia extensions.

OS/9: (Operating System/9) Operating system originally developed for the Motorola 6809 processor in the late Seventies, and was used widely on microcomputers based on the 6809 and subsequent processors of Motorola family. Micros include the Tandy Colour Computer, Atari ST and the Dragon 32/64. Because CDI is based on a Motorola processor, OS/9 was adopted and modified for Philips' purposes, calling it CD-RTOS (Compact Disc - Real-Time Operating System).

Overlay: Placement of one screen image on top of another. In CDI, using transparency, one image plane can be laid over another. It often applies to mixing computer generated images with video using a genlock.

PAL: (Phase Alternating Line) Video standard developed in West Germany, delivering 50 fields/25 frames per second on the 625 line system. Used in the UK, much of Europe, Africa, Australia and South America.

Path/Trail: Path followed through series of linked nodes in hypertext or hypermedia material.

PCMCIA: (Personal Computer Memory Card International Association) Slots which connect with almost credit card size peripheral devices. The exact dimensions of a PCMCIA card are, 8.5cm * 5.5cm, and their thickness may be either 3.3mm, 5mm or 10.5mm. Memory cards are 3.3mm thick, I/O devices are 5mm thick and hard disks are 10.5mm thick.

The original PCMCIA was designed for memory cartridges only, but in September 1991 the PCMCIA Type II (PCMCIA 2.0) specification was launched facilitating hard disks and modem/facsimile devices. : However, though the PCMCIA laid down a hardware specification for slots and cards it did not specify a software interface, so some PCMCIA cards are proprietary. To solve this Intel introduced a standard interchangeable card aimed at Intel based machines. Called Exchangeable Card Architecture (ExCA), third-party manufacturers are free to use the logo provided their cards ExCA compliant.

Pentium: Intel's successor to the 486 processor.

PhotoCD: A CD variant developed by Kodak in conjunction with Philips, and launched in 1992, PhotoCD permits the processing of 35mm photographic negatives into digital form. Kodak continues to licence high-street photographic finishers to develop conventional film reels into images on PhotoCD using a CD-R drive. Additional films can be processed and added to the same PhotoCD on up to 99 different occasions (99 being the maximum number of tracks supported). Following the addition of the second batch of images, it becomes a 'multisession' CD.

Photographs can be stored at a number of different resolutions, including 128 by 192, 256 by 384, 512 by 768, 1024 by 1536 and 2048 by 3072. Images of up to 18Mb can be compressed down to 4.5Mb without noticeable loss of quality.

Together with appropriate software, images on PhotoCD can be viewed using dedicated PhotoCD players, CD-ROM XA compatible drives, so-called XA-ready drives, CD-I players and multi-session CD-ROM drives. PhotoCDs can be read using conventional CD-ROM drives, but only one 'session' can be accessed and viewed. It should also be noted that XA-ready drives are not 100% CD-ROM XA compatible as many require additional interface circuitry to read interleaved data, which is the central theme of CD-ROM XA. Basically current XA-ready drives lack the ADPCM (Adaptive Delta Pulse Code Modulation) (See Chapter 3).

In addition to Kodak PhotoCD Access, Corel Draw, MS Word, Adobe PhotoShop, Shoebox and PhotoEdge are just some of many other software products able to open and read PhotoCD images. The future PhotoCD standard will be a multimedia one, where interleaved audio will be included, giving the ability to tag sound bites to images. Taking advantage of this development, it will be necessary to have a delivery system that incorporates ADPCM (See Chapter 3) circuitry.

Pioneer DRM-604X: Multi-play CD-ROM drive specified as producing a continuous 600Kbytes/sec data transfer rate. In independent tests (See Chapter 2), the DRM-604X transferred 60Mbytes in a staggering 10 seconds, giving an average data transfer rate of 598Kbytes/sec

Pixel: Images are composed of a number of dots (pixels). On CRTs, pixels physically consist of red, green and blue phosphor deposits.

PostScript: Industry standard language for driving printers; printers must be of PostScript variety for reproduction of PostScript files.

Procedural: Languages such as C and Pascal require a number of statements to implement all decision making processes (*See Fourth Generation and Fifth Generation*).

Processor (CPU): Comprises numerous registers, including a program counter used to point at the next memory location from which memory addresses, instructions or data are retrieved. Also consists of an Arithmetic Logic Unit (ALU) responsible for arithmetic and logic operations. (Overall internal design can be dissected much further.) Numerous external connections include a data bus and an address bus. 'N' data lines (internally as well as externally) corresponds to 'n' bit processor. Reference to the CPU of a microcomputer such as IBM PS/2 or Apple Macintosh as a processor is technically incorrect. Such CPUs are accommodated on a single chip of silicon (but possible using other semiconductor materials), and are strictly microprocessors. Research and development (1991 - Anomartic Cambridge, UK) clearly indicates that, theoretically, more than one chip may be used to accommodate more complex CPUs using wafer-scale or whole-scale integration, where a larger portion of wafer is united to produce a single multiple chip, but single circuit, device.

PROM: (Programmable Read Only Memory) Read-only electronic memory used to store firmware.

QuickTime: Standard video compression software for the Apple Macintosh (See Chapter 3).

Real-time: Program or system which operates in real-time regurgitates data, or responds to user interaction, instantly; program or system which captures and/or compresses data at the rate it actually occurs - for example a live satellite broadcast link is in real-time.

Red Book Standard: World-wide standard for encoding conventional audio CDs. Sometimes referred to as Red Track Audio.

Removable Medium: Medium such as floppy disk, CD-ROM, CDI disc which can be removed from a drive or system.

RGB: (Red Green Blue) - Computer monitor output where each colour component red, green and blue is represented by an individual signal. Range of colours which can be generated depends upon how many bits are used to represent each (primary) colour component. For example 8-bit RGB where 256 (2^8) shades of each colour component are possible, gives a total of over 16.7 million (256 * 256 * 256) colours.

RGB (5:5:5): (Red Green Blue 5:5:5) - Technique used in CDI giving 5-bit RGB where each colour component may be excited to produce one of 32 shades, giving a total of 32,768 (32 * 32 * 32) colours.

RLC: (Run Length Coding) - Loss-less compression process. Often used in conjunction with DCT and forms part of the JPEG algorithm *(See Chapter 3)*. Most effective for cartoon-like images, permitting full-screen, motion sequences in CDI.

ROM: (Read Only Memory) - Electronic memory from which it is only possible to read data *(See EAROM, EPROM and PROM)*.

Root Directory: Top-level directory in storage medium in which all other sub-directories, directly or indirectly, find their roots.

RS232: Recommended Standard by Electronic Industries Association (EIA) for the serial transmission of data over relatively short distances, but greater than those internal to most computer systems. Standard representation of digital data, using TTL for example, is limited in terms of transmission distance. To overcome this, signal strength is broadly increased. RS232 represents an industry standard for achieving this, so as to increase transmission distance, and give interchangeability of computer peripherals.

S-VHS: (Super-VHS) - Enhanced variant of VHS video tape standard. Luminance and chrominance are encoded separately, giving improved picture quality.

Sample: Digital sound sequence derived from analogue source. (See Sampling Rate.)

Sampling Rate: Frequency at which incoming signal is sampled for processing purposes. The sampling rate of an ADC influences effectiveness of conversion.

Scanner: Device used to digitise photographic material or art work. Either hand-held or flat-bed. With optical character recognition (OCR) software, can be used to convert text into machine readable form.

Script: Series of instructions which can be interpreted by a program. Sometimes referred to as macros. Scripts can be generated through menu selections or programming lines of code.

Script-based environment: Multimedia authoring system/environment which requires extensive program sequences or scripts. Generally difficult to use for non-programmers. Current trends indicate a departure from this approach toward systems which require little or no programming skills.

SCSI: (Small Computer System Interface) - Universal and internationally agreed interface standard backed by ANSI (American National Standards Institute), intended to provide interchangeability between peripherals and computer systems from different manufacturers. It is not intended solely for the attachment of CD-ROM drives, and is often used to interface hard disk drives and scanners. Apple Computer have long since realised the importance of SCSI fitting Macintosh machines with appropriate controllers. SCSI interface cards can be fitted to a PC XT/AT or PS/2 (or compatibles). Up to seven SCSI drive (or compatible peripheral) can be connected using standard implementations.

SECAM: (Systeme Electronique Coleur Avec Memoire) - Broadcast television standard used in France, and in many parts of Eastern Europe. Like PAL, it runs at 25 frame/50 fields per second in the 625 line system.

Second Generation Language: Where instructions are represented by concise mnemonics, the language is said to be a second generation language. Such 'assembly languages' are indigenous to processors. Common example include 6809, 6502, Z80 and 68000 versions. The terms assembly language and machine code are regarded as interchangeable.

Serial Port: Input/output port through which data is transmitted/received sequentially. RS232 is a standard serial port used to transmit serial digital information over modest distances so as to connect communication devices and other serial peripherals to computers.

SoftPC^{R}: From Insignia Solutions, PC (MS-DOS) emulation program for Apple Macintosh.

Sound card: Generally a plug-in card which permits sampling, multi-voice sound synthesis and speech synthesis (See Chapter 3).

SoundBlaster: Range of sound cards produced by Creative Technology.

Sprite: Screen image confined to limited number of pixels, often used as 'characters' in computer games, and pointers in DTP programs. Highly mobile, they may be defined by hardware or software.

SRAM: (Static Random Access Memory) - Volatile form of electronic memory which is not constantly refreshed. It therefore consumes less power.

Stack: Area of electronic memory preserved for the temporary storage of memory addresses, instructions and data. It is a LIFO *(See LIFO)* system. In HyperCard parlance a Stack refers to a collection of 'cards', which represent complete applications.

Still Video Camera: Colour photographic images (slides or prints) or art work can be digitised using a still video camera. Operates by writing images in analogue form to a two inch diameter magnetic, (video) floppy disc that can store up to 50 exposures. Using a still video player, exposures can be digitised using a frame grabber or video capture board.

StoryBoard (Plus/Live): Hypermedia/hypertext authoring tool from IBM widely used for presentations. Runs on IBM PC family of computers with EGA or VGA graphics.

Sub notebook: Portable computer considerably smaller and lighter than conventional notebook computers.

Super Beta: Enhanced Beta videotape variant, using 0.5'' tape.

SuperDrive^{TM}: Multiple standard Macintosh drive able to read Apple Macintosh (400 Kbytes, 800 Kbytes and 1.44 Mbytes) disks, MS-DOS, OS/2 (720 Kbytes and 1.44 Mbytes) disks and ProDOS (Apple II) disks.

Tape Streamer: Magnetic tape storage device used to backup hard disk data as a contingency measure against data loss or data corruption resulting from system failure or interruption in power supply. Data recovery simply involves copying the contents of the tape streamer to a functioning hard disk.

Third Generation Language: High level languages such as Pascal, BASIC and C are third generation languages. They are procedural languages in that actions have to specified and implemented through procedures (*See First Generation, Second Generation, Fifth Generation and 4GL*).

Timeline: Method of linking nodes in hypertext or hypermedia material according to chronological order. For example, a hypermedia encyclopedia may link documents according to date.

ToolBook: Product of Asymetrix Corporation, a hypermedia authoring tool for the PC running Windows 3. In many ways, except in terms of indigenous terminology, it is a HyperCard clone. It can be assumed to be slower than HyperCard.

Transputer: Inmos parallel processor for the creation of parallel processing systems. Commercial transputer-based systems include the ATW (Atari Transputer Workstation). High-end system which harnesses more fully the transputer/parallel processing concept is the Meiko Computing Surface. Several Transputers exist including the T212, T414, T800 and T900. Division (Bristol, UK) apply transputer technology to virtual reality. Parallel processing concept, theoretically offers a great deal in many areas, including AI (artificial intelligence), sophisticated computer models, as well as virtual reality and multimedia. Its effectiveness so far, however, has been limited because of lack of third-party transputer-based, system manufacturers.

TTL: (Transistor Transistor Logic) - Standard representation used in logic devices and in systems, denoting digital data. Consumes relatively large amount of current.

Turnkey System: System which is made fully operational by vendor, usually on site. Turnkey suppliers.

Typed Link: Originally described in a thesis by Randall Trigg, can be defined and annotated with descriptions of relationships between associated node objects. With consistent vocabulary, the model becomes more manageable and more easily maintained.

Unix: Multi-tasking operating system originally developed at Bell Laboratories for the creation of inter-departmental reports. It has since evolved into numerous commercial variants including Xenix, which is often thought of as the PC face of Unix. Workstations run Unix. Santa Cruz Operation (SCO) are commonly associated with Unix. Existing versions of Unix are quite different at the code level.

UPS: (Uninterruptable Power Supply) - Device which prevents data loss following power supply failure or deviation.

UI: (User Interface) Software module or program through which user interacts with one or more applications *(See GUI)*.

V: One of two chrominance components of colour video signal.

Vertical market: Specialist or niche market

VGA: (Video Graphics Array) - Graphics standard released in mid 1987 by IBM as part of its PS/2 range. Many non-standard variants now exist *(See Chapter 3)*. Typical pixel resolutions include 640 by 400, 800 by 600 and 1,024 by 768. 8 or 16 bit adapter cards (often autosensing) often have from 256 Kbytes to 1 Mbyte of VRAM. The latter supports 768 by 1,024 pixels resolution in 256 colours. Trident is a popular VGA chip set. Cards are sometimes switchable between interlaced and non-interlaced modes.

VHS: (Video Home System) - Standard 0.5'' video cassette developed by Matsushita and JVC. Successful in forcing BetaMax standard out of VCR market.

Video Capture Board: Means to capture and sometimes compress motion video and convert it into digital form.

Video for Windows: Microsoft Video for Windows (VfW) is a response to Apple QuickTime, which has quickly become a de facto software standard for producing motion video in the Macintosh environment. VfW permits video play-back, capture and editing. Minimum PC requirements is an MPC specified machine. A 486-based MPC can yield near FMPSV (Full Motion Part Sreen Video) covering quarter of the screen and running at 25fps. With a video delivery device fitted, such as those based upon the Intel i750 chipset, video running at up to 30fps is possible. Video clips can be added to applications through OLE (Object Linking and Embedding). For example, video clips can be added to Lotus Ami Pro, MS Word, MS Excel, Lotus Notes, and a growing number of others. Video capture requires an appropriate video capture board and 30MHz 386-based system. Also included is a means of converting QuickTime into the VfW format. VfW supports the AVI (Audio Video Interleaved) format and has an installable Codec interface.

VideoBlaster: Low cost video recorder produced by Creative Technology.

Videodisc: Disc used to store video images. Nowadays has come to mean an optically encoded disc, but need not necessarily depend upon optical techniques. 12 cm videodisc players are commercially available.

Virtual Reality: Full immersion virtual reality (VR) is a concept by which monitor screen is replaced by helmet, or HMD (Head Mount Display), or EyePhone™, containing LCD displays and headphones. A wide angle of vision is simulated within which 3D images are generated. The user is able to move within environment using special hand signals made recognisable by wearing a DataGlove™ - usually Lycra glove fitted with optic sensors - also possible to wear complete suit. Sound is made more authentic using AudioSphere™ which produces 3D sound rendering and so provides sound/audio relative to user's location in any given virtual world.

Applications include leisure simulators, flight simulators, land vehicle simulators and many types of CAD including architectural, car prototyping and other 3D structures, as well as robotics. Virtual reality allows complex 3D models to be experienced and studied. VPL Research (Redwood City, CA) produce an array of related hardware. Division (Bristol, UK) offer transputer-based hardware able to interface with VPL peripherals, and harness the concept mainly for robotics. Transputers ideally suited to this application as the necessary processing power is yielded to carry out great number of control functions. Division's system also makes use of Intel i860 for graphics purposes which when introduced into the design made several transputers redundant; multi-user system expandable to 300 users.

Volatile RAM: (Volatile Random Access Memory) Conventional SRAM or DRAM unable to maintain stored data following interruption of power supply.

WIMP: (Windows, Icons, Mouse and Pop-up menus) Traditional acronym for GUI environment such as HyperCard, Presentation Manager and Windows.

Windows 3.x (Microsoft): Multi-tasking environment with GUI for PC with 286 or better. Requires one Mbyte of memory, though at least two Mbytes are recommended.

Windows for Workgroups: Network version of Windows.

Windows 3.0 Multimedia Extensions: Set of extensions for windows which provide a multimedia delivery environment (See Chapter 3). Supplied as standard with Windows 3.x (or higher).

WORM drive: (Write Once, Read Many) - Device to which data may be written but not erased or overwritten.

WORM medium: (Write Once, Read Many) - Media to which data may be written but not erased or overwritten.

WYSIWYG: (What-you-see-is-what-you-get) - Term applied to a program which is capable of generating on screen exactly what will be printed. Often programs claimed to be WYSIWYG offer a means of reviewing what will be ultimately printed. In such cases it is not possible to edit WYSIWYG screen images.

Y: Luminance component of video signal.

YUV: Collective name given to luminance (Y) and chrominance components of video signal.

Index

Exclusive Money-Saving CD-ROM Offer:

aneCDote

– the CD-ROM magazine from Nimbus Information Systems

As a reader of 'Multimedia on Your PC', you can buy a copy of this information-packed and entertaining CD-ROM which normally retails at £10 FOR ONLY £5 (plus £1 p&p),

Orders to:

Nimbus Manufacturing (UK) Ltd
CD-ROM Division
Llantarman Park
Cwmbran
Gwent NP44 3AB

Books from Sigma Press

Sigma publish a wide range of books under three imprints:

Sigma Science: popular science

'*Alice in Quantumland*' is the first, with *'Birth of the Box'* - a fascinating history of the development of television, demonstrating how technology can be developed into a marketable commodity. Human interest abounds - did the Russians invent TV? The coming of colour; Satellite TV and future developments. Due in Spring 1994.

Sigma Press: for computing and technology

- ❑ Accountancy and other business applications
- ❑ Acorn, Amiga, Amstrad and Atari
- ❑ Beginners' guides
- ❑ Communications and networking
- ❑ Computer games and entertainment
- ❑ Hardware and architecture
- ❑ Mid-range computers
- ❑ Multimedia
- ❑ Operating systems
- ❑ Programming

Sigma Leisure: outdoor and cultural activities

- ❑ Cycling and mountain biking
- ❑ Hill walking
- ❑ Military history
- ❑ Regional heritage
- ❑ Myths and legends

All of our books are available from your usual bookshop, or direct from:

SIGMA PRESS,
1 SOUTH OAK LANE,
WILMSLOW, CHESHIRE, SK9 6AR

PHONE: 0625 – 531035; FAX: 0625 – 536800

Complete catalogues available